DISCOVERY
A Challenge to Teachers

PRENTICE-HALL SERIES IN CURRICULUM AND TEACHING

Ronald T. Hyman, Consulting Editor

DISCOVERY
A Challenge to Teachers

HAROLD MORINE and GRETA MORINE

PRENTICE-HALL, INC., ENGLEWOOD CLIFFS, NEW JERSEY

Library of Congress Cataloging in Publication Data

MORINE, HAROLD
   Discovery: a challenge to teachers.

   (Prentice-Hall series in curriculum and teaching)
   Bibliography: p.
   1. Learning by discovery. I. Morine, Greta,
joint author. II. Title.
LB1067.M72   372.1'3'9   72-5851
ISBN 0-13-215954-6
ISBN 0-13-215947-3 (pbk.)

© 1973 by Prentice-Hall, Inc., Englewood Cliffs, New Jersey

10 9 8 7 6 5 4 3 2 1

PRINTED IN THE UNITED STATES OF AMERICA

Prentice-Hall International, Inc., London
Prentice-Hall of Australia, Pty. Ltd., Sydney
Prentice-Hall of Canada, Ltd., Toronto
Prentice-Hall of India Private Limited, New Delhi
Prentice-Hall of Japan, Inc., Tokyo

To all the teachers who challenged us,
and most particularly to
DAN ROSELLE, BILL KNODE, RAY SCHEELE,
LELAND JACOBS, AND DWAYNE HUEBNER

Contents

Preface

This book is the result of ten years of discovery on the part of the authors: discovering how to use inductive techniques with elementary school children; discovering how to produce instructional materials based on inductive procedures; discovering how to train preservice and in-service teachers to use inductive techniques. We have been frequently delighted by the exciting discovery lessons we have observed our students teach, and we have often commiserated with them over discovery lessons that turned into disaster. In the process of analyzing both types of lessons, we have learned a great deal about discovery methods.

Many of the materials in this book have been very effectively used with our students for four years. Many of the sample lessons have been produced and tested by our students. They are presented here in a format that involves the reader in some independent inquiry. Throughout much of the book the following sequence is repeated: interaction with materials, production of ideas, explanations, or plans by the reader; comparison of productions by several readers; presentation of sample productions by the authors, together with analysis, for additional comparison by the reader. In short this book is designed to encourage *active* reading.

Essentially, this text is a *practical* approach to discovery methods, with tested suggestions on how to proceed. However, we strongly believe that a well-understood theory is the most practical tool a teacher can have. Therefore, our practical suggestions are always related to theoretical considerations, which are explained at intervals throughout the book.

We are indebted to the many students who have used these materials for their help in refining and improving them, to Rob Spaulding for his comments on an early form of the manuscript, and to Esther Vigil for her suggestions on format. We also are grateful to the students who have permitted us to use their ideas for sample lessons. They are mentioned by name in footnotes throughout the text. It is our earnest hope that readers of this text will become as adept in use of discovery methods as did these students.

HANK AND GRETA MORINE

DISCOVERY
A Challenge to Teachers

PART I

A CHALLENGE
TO THINK FOR YOURSELF

Teaching by discovery is not a new method of instruction. The Herbartian inductive lesson, an early ancestor of the modern discovery lesson, was in vogue in the early 1900s. The Dewey problem-solving approach, another forerunner, had its greatest swell of popularity in the 1930s. The modern versions of the discovery method have been frequently discussed in educational journals since 1960, and instructional materials utilizing discovery techniques have been increasing steadily in number since 1963.

Why, then, is the incidence of teachers in the public schools who use the discovery method still notably low? After expending several years of effort on training both preservice and in-service teachers in the use of discovery techniques, the authors have come to the conclusion that many teachers have been handicapped in their attempts to use discovery methods by the fact that they themselves have rarely had an opportunity to learn by discovery.

Teachers who lack personal experience in logical problem solving by the inductive method find it difficult to anticipate the problems that children might have. They underestimate children's ability to perceive materials in divergent ways, and unexpected responses during a lesson may throw them off balance.

We have found that teachers who try some inductive discovery of their own, before attempting to use the method with children, are much more confident and effective. They also tend to be more aware of the various factors that can affect children's ability to generalize.

The first three chapters of this book are designed to give the reader some experience in inductive thinking, to indicate some procedural differences between inductive discovery lessons and more direct or deductive lessons, and to explore the effects of different materials on the inductive process. The approach used is basically an inductive one, so far as this is possible in book form. The reader is presented with data or information and asked to respond to certain questions relative to the data. At a later point, some possible answers to the questions are presented for consideration. The reader is urged to record his own responses to the questions before reading the presentation of possible answers. We realize that this is a more time-consuming activity, but we are convinced that the additional insights into what is taking place in the learner's head while he is involved in the act of discovering that are gained as a result will be well worth the time and effort.

chapter 1

Comparing Two Lessons

Most teachers are familiar with various kinds of teaching procedures, or teaching "strategies," in modern parlance. There is some evidence that the most effective teachers are those who utilize a variety of procedures or strategies in their daily teaching.[1]

It is sometimes difficult to compare teaching strategies in terms of classroom interaction, because few teachers attempt to teach the same concept in two different ways. This is unfortunate, because there is much to be learned from such a comparison.

On the pages which follow are lesson plans and transcriptions of two lessons, both of which were taught to fourth-grade children of about

---

QUESTIONS TO CONSIDER

The reader is asked to study the two lessons and to answer the following questions:

In what ways are the two lesson plans alike? How do they differ? Consider objectives, materials, procedures, and evaluation.

What differences do you notice in the things the teacher does in Lesson A as compared with Lesson B?

What differences do you notice in what the children do in the two lessons?

What differences do you notice in the amount of content covered in the two lessons?

What differences do you notice in the information on the blackboard at the end of the two lessons?

---

1 Ned Flanders and Anita Simon, "Teacher Effectiveness," in *Encyclopedia of Educational Research*, ed. Robert L. Ebel, American Educational Research Association (Toronto: Collier-Macmillan Ltd., 1969), p. 1428.

average ability. Both lessons deal with sentence types (statements, questions, and commands). Both lessons were taught by the same teacher. The lessons differ in the kinds of teaching procedures used.

LESSON A

LESSON PLAN

OBJECTIVES

Children will identify several differences between statements, questions, and commands
Children will independently rewrite and transform one kind of sentence into another
Children will develop skills in observing and generalizing

MATERIALS

Sentences on blackboard
Worksheets [*see Fig. 1–1*]

PROCEDURES

1. Write on board:

1	2	3
Jean is going to the movie.	Is Jean going to the movie?	Go to the movie.
John finished his homework.	Did John finish his homework?	Finish your homework.
The boy hit the ball.	Did the boy hit the ball?	Hit the ball.
She is washing the dishes.	Is she washing the dishes?	Wash the dishes.
José will mow the lawn.		
You can tell a funny joke.		
	Can you catch the cat?	
	Did Maria buy a new dress?	
		Eat your vegetables.
		Close the door.

2. Have children read sentences aloud moving across the board. Ask them to fill in the blanks, so that there are three sets of ten sentences each. As sentences are given, ask class if they agree with the wording. Write the sentences on the board.
3. Ask children to write down a sentence that will go in each column.

Have them do this on papers at their seats. Have children read their examples to the class. Ask if others agree that they belong in the proposed column. If they disagree, have them reword sentence so it does fit. Write the sentences on the board, in the appropriate column.

4. Ask children what differences they see between the three groups of sentences. How are the sentences in each group alike? How are they different from the other groups? Write their answers on the board. If children do not give the information, ask if anyone knows the names for these types of sentences.

5. Give children worksheet [*Fig. 1–1*] to do.

EVALUATION

What differences are children able to identify?
How many children could transform sentences appropriately?
How accurately do they handle the worksheet?

WORKSHEET

Name _____   Date _____

Tell what kind of sentence each of the following is. Write *S* for statement, *Q* for question, or *C* for command.

_____ 1. Get out your reading books.
_____ 2. Did you put your name on the top of the paper?
_____ 3. Nancy likes to write stories.
_____ 4. Did you wash your hands?
_____ 5. Set the table.
_____ 6. Turn off the TV.
_____ 7. The boy got into the car.
_____ 8. Can you run a mile?
_____ 9. Were you late for school?
_____10. I will take a nap.

Fig. 1–1

BLACKBOARD AT END OF LESSON A

Jean is going to the movie.	Is Jean going to the movie?	Go to the movie.
John finished his homework.	Did John finish his homework?	Finish your homework.
The boy hit the ball.	Did the boy hit the ball?	Hit the ball.
She is washing the dishes.	Is she washing the dishes?	Wash the dishes.

BLACKBOARD AT END OF LESSON A (Cont.)

(José) will mow the lawn.	Will (José) mow the lawn?	Mow the lawn.
(You) can tell a funny joke.	Can (you) tell a funny joke?	Tell a funny joke.
(You) can catch the cat.	Can (you) catch the cat?	Catch the cat.
(Maria) bought a new dress.	Did (Maria) buy a new dress?	Buy a new dress.
(You) will eat your vegetables.	Will (you) eat your vegetables?	Eat your vegetables.
(You) closed the door.	Did (you) close the door?	Close the door.
(He) is outside playing.	Is (he) outside playing?	Be outside playing.
(We) are in Fremont.	Are (we) in Fremont?	Be in Fremont.
(You) can run fast.	Can (you) run fast?	Run fast.
(I) am at the store.		
(I) like that horse.		
	Are (you) going to the lake?	Go to the lake.
	Will (you) move the furniture?	
		Catch a snake.
		Ride the horse.
		Make a machine.

"Be" words in middle. Subject in beginning. You don't have to answer or do anything. Called STATEMENTS	Question mark at end. "Be" words in beginning. Subject in middle. You answer it. Called QUESTIONS	Not as many words. Where is the subject? You do something. Called COMMANDS (orders, demands)

Fig. 1–2

SAMPLE OF CLASSROOM CONVERSATION—LESSON A

T (teacher): Can you tell me some of the ways that all the sentences in column 2 are alike?

Tammy: They're all questions.

T: How many would agree with that?

(Children raise hands.)

Carl: There's one up there that doesn't have a question mark after it, though.

T: Carl said something about the ending of these sentences. What's true about the ending of them?

Steve: They all have question marks, except where you forgot to put one in. . . .

T: Anything else that would help us tell column 2 apart from the other two columns? Judy?

Judy: They're using the "be" words.

T: What "be" words?

Judy: Like "are" and "is."

T: Where are we using them?

Judy: "*Is* he outside playing?" "*Are* we in Fremont?"

T: (*Underlining "are" and "is."*) Can you find these words in any of the other sentences in column 2?

(*Children indicate others.*)

T: So we have several sentences with "is" and "are." What about those sentences? How are they alike? Mike?

Mike: You mean the "be" words? Some of them are at the beginning and some of them are in the middle.

T: Where are they in the middle of the sentence?

Mark: My cat is going away.

(*T. underlines "is" in that sentence.*)

T: Now we've found several sentences that have "be" words in the middle. What can we say about all these sentences?

Steve: They're in column 1.

T: What about the "be" words in the sentences in column 2?

Marcia: They're in the beginning.

T: All right. That's one difference between column 1 and column 2. We have "be" words in the beginning in column 2, and we have "be" words in the middle in column 1. (*Writes this on board.*) . . .

T: What's the subject in this sentence [*points to "Is Jean going to the movies?"*]?

Children: "Jean."

(*T. circles "Jean," continues down column 2, and circles subject of each sentence as children identify it.*)

T: Now let's look for the subjects of the sentences in column 1. (*Goes through same process of circling subject as children identify it.*)

T: Now what's different between the two columns?

Several children: I know, I know! . . .

T: Now I have a very tough question. Who can tell me where the subjects are in column 3?

Carl: There aren't any.

T: What? Carl says there aren't any! Marcia?

Marcia: At the end.

T: Marcia says they're at the end.

Several children: Yeah, yeah.

T: Let's look at the first sentence: "Jean is going to the movie." We said "Jean" was the subject, and it was at the beginning. And in column 2 we have "Is Jean going to the movie?" and we said "Jean" was the subject, and it was in the middle. The third column says, "Go to the movie."

Paul: Well, "Jean" is the subject, but she isn't there anymore.

T: Jean got left out, didn't she? She disappeared.

(*Children laugh.*)

T: Well, it's a hard question, but I'm not going to tell you the answer. We'll see if you can figure it out some day.

(*General conversation for a minute as children argue with each other over point.*)

LESSON B

LESSON PLAN

OBJECTIVES

Children will identify statements, questions, and commands

MATERIALS

Sentences on blackboard
Worksheet [*see Fig. 1–1*]

PROCEDURES

1. Write on board:

1	2	3
Jean is going to the movie.	Is Jean going to the movie?	Go to the movie.

(1)	(2)	(3)
John finished his homework.	Did John finish his homework?	Finish your homework.
The boy hit the ball.	Did the boy hit the ball?	Hit the ball.
She is washing the dishes.	Is she washing the dishes?	Wash the dishes.

2. Explain that there are three kinds of sentences on the board. Have children read them aloud. Ask if they know what the sentences are called. Identify them as statements, questions, and commands. Tell children how the three types are different:

Punctuation: 1—period; 2—question mark; 3—period
Response of listener: 1—just listens; 2—gives an answer; 3—performs an action
Structure: 1—subject/predicate; 2—predicate/subject/predicate; 3—predicate only

3. Have children identify the subjects and predicates in the sentences to make sure they see the structure.
4. Write group of new sentences on board, and have children identify them as statements, questions, or commands. Have them check each sentence to make sure it has the characteristics identified above.
5. Give children worksheet [*Fig. 1–1*] to do.

EVALUATION

Can children identify the new group of sentences accurately as statements, questions, or commands?
Can children do worksheet accurately?

BLACKBOARD AT END OF LESSON B

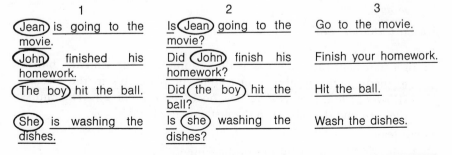

1	2	3
(Jean) is going to the movie.	Is (Jean) going to the movie?	Go to the movie.
(John) finished his homework.	Did (John) finish his homework?	Finish your homework.
(The boy) hit the ball.	Did (the boy) hit the ball?	Hit the ball.
(She) is washing the dishes.	Is (she) washing the dishes?	Wash the dishes.

	STATEMENTS	QUESTIONS	COMMANDS
Punctuation:	Period	Question mark	Period
Reaction:	Listen; don't have to talk	Answer the question	Obey the command
Subject:	At beginning	In middle	Not stated
Predicate:	At end	Split; part at beginning, part at end	Whole sentence

S 1. José will mow the lawn.
C 2. Eat your vegetables.
Q 3. Can you catch the cat?
C 4. Close the door.
S 5. You can tell a funny joke.
Q 6. Did Maria buy a new dress?

Fig. 1–3

SAMPLE OF CLASSROOM CONVERSATION—LESSON B

T (*teacher*): There are ways we can tell the difference between a statement, a question, and a command. One way to tell is punctuation. What punctuation is used here on the end of a statement? (*Points to column 1 sentences.*)

Tom: Periods.

T: Right. (*Writes "period" on board by column 1.*) . . .

T: In a statement the predicate is at the end of the sentence. (*Writes "predicate at end" on board by column 1.*) A question is very different. The predicate in a question is split in two. Let me show you in the first question. Here's the predicate, part at the beginning and part at the end. (*Underlines predicate of "Is Jean going to the movie?"*)

Several Children: Oh! . . .

T: In a statement the subject is at the beginning of the sentence, but in a question, the subject is in a different place. It's in the middle. (*Writes "subject in middle" on board by column 2.*) Who thinks they can find the subject in the first sentence here? Tom?

Tom: Jean.

T: Right. And it's in the middle of the sentence. . . .

T: The interesting thing about a command is that the subject is not stated. (*Writes "subject not stated" on board by column 3.*) The subject is the person that you're giving the command to, really. If you're talking to Jean, and you say, "Go to the movie," Jean is the person who's supposed to do the action. But we don't say that in the sentence. We *understand* it because we know who we're talking to. So those are very special kinds of sentences. The subject isn't stated. . . .

T: There's another way that helps us tell the difference, and that is the reaction. Reaction is what you *do* when somebody else does something. The kind of thing that you do when somebody asks a question is—

Karen: —answer.

T: —is answer it. Good. (*Writes "answer question" on board by column 2.*) What is your reaction when someone gives you a command? Bobby?

Bobby: You obey.

T: You obey the command, or you do it. Yes.

EAVESDROPPING ON A DISCUSSION

Having studied the two lessons and considered your own answers to the five questions suggested for comparison, you may find it interesting to eavesdrop on a discussion of the same two lessons. The discussants are preservice students in a teacher training program on the West Coast. You can "listen" to their comments on each question in turn, and compare them with your own.

How are the two lesson plans alike?

Student A: The only things I saw alike were the subject matter and the sentences written on the worksheet and the blackboard.

Student B: The materials were the same, but Lesson A had more examples.

Student D: Did you notice how much more open the examples looked in Lesson A? I mean, all those blank spaces were just asking you to do something.

Student C: But that's a difference. We're talking about likenesses now. One likeness was that in both lessons the evaluations matched the objectives. Like, in B, the objective was to have them learn and the evaluation was: Did they learn? And in A she asks: How many children can transform sentences properly? Well she would know by watching what they did in class, and they would have to think to do it.

D: But in A she has more *ways* to evaluate it. In B she only has the worksheet, because she doesn't get enough responses from the children in the lesson.

How are the two lesson plans different?

A: The objectives are different.

B: In Plan A you had *more* objectives.

C: One of the objectives in Lesson A was to have more student response.

D: The objectives in A were so much more, ah, ambitious—I guess that's the word I want.

B: I thought after reading the evaluation for Lesson A that there was more emphasis on what the children could not do. It wasn't just what *can* they do. When you ask, "How many children could transform sentences appropriately?" you sort of say that probably some can't, and you're paying attention to that. In Lesson B the evaluation question is "Can children identify. . . ." It sort of suggests that if one can, they all can.

A: Lesson B seemed more concrete, more definite to me.

B: Well in Lesson B she knew definitely what she wanted to say.

A: Lesson B seemed organized, too.

C: I thought A was organized. They seemed to cover the same material and subject, but they went off in different directions.

A: If I was a kid I would probably get more confused in A than I would in B.

D: Where would you be confused? Maybe at the beginning. But once you started doing it you'd understand more.

C: I think what you're saying is that the format was different. I thought it was really interesting how at the end the blackboards looked so different. It was like when you learn something by yourself—Lesson A was like that—like if you're reading about something new, your first overall picture is, "What is it?" You don't understand it. It's confusing. But at the end you can state your new knowledge.

What differences do you notice in the things the teacher does?

A: In Lesson B she talks more.

B: Didn't Lesson B remind you of a lecture in college?

D: It seemed to me that most of the lessons I've ever had have been like B.

C: It wasn't just talking *more*, because in Lesson A she asked and in Lesson B she told.

D: In Lesson B she explains things more. But in Lesson A she just left it up in the air.

A: I didn't like that at all.

B: I didn't either, but that's not what we're discussing.

C: I think in Lesson A what she was trying to do was to get the kids to think about it for a while.

A: But I wouldn't have ended it without telling them. Because I remember it was hard to understand that kind of sentence.

D: Well the only thing I can figure is she wanted the kids to think about it, because sometimes when you figure it out for yourself you remember it better.

A: That's what the point was, but when I want an answer, I need it then. And little kids do too.

B: What other differences were there in what she did?

D: In A the teacher got her direction from the kids. They'd say something, and she'd ask, "What do you mean," and they'd go on from there.

C: In Lesson A the teacher asked questions that helped kids find their own answers.

B: The questions the teacher asked in B were all the right-wrong type. But in A they were discussion questions.

C: Yes, and in A all the children's answers were treated as valid.

D: Well in Lesson A she asked other children if they agreed with the answer, but in B *she* said you're right or wrong.

What differences do you notice in what the children do?

A: In Lesson B the children have to listen.

B: In Lesson A the children have to be more analytical.

C: In A the children had to think up the sentences. In B they just read the ones the teacher made up.

B: The children talked more in Lesson A.

D: They're really involved in the whole thing.

C: Also they're writing. They're writing down sentences, and they're making up the rules to go on the blackboard.

A: In Lesson A the children had a lot of discussion among themselves.

It was a lot noisier classroom. The attention wasn't always on the teacher.

C: But the kids in Lesson A asked questions. I thought that was neat.

B: Yeah, but she didn't answer them. I think that after a while they'd get tired of asking them.

D: Well they had to think more in Lesson A. A seems to be building on what the children already know. B doesn't build at all—just "boom," there it is.

C: You could say that A is more developmental.

What differences do you notice in the amount of content covered?

A: She was using the child's terminology in Lesson A. But I think she ought to make sure that everyone understood what the child meant. I mean, predicates aren't just "be" words.

C: The thing is, all these sentences don't have "be" words in them.

B: Maybe after the children really understood it she could go back and show them the other predicate words and tell them what they're called.

A: Lesson B covers the subject in much more detail. Lesson A is much broader.

C: But also in Lesson A the children are getting practice in changing the different types of sentences.

D: The content in A is about the same as in Lesson B, but the kids are learning to think in Lesson A. Isn't that a kind of content too?

C: I think there's less covered in the second lesson. It's a shorter lesson. Look at the objectives.

D: In B she was trying to get a specific skill across. But in A she was interested in getting at the possibility of generating your own concepts.

B: Are you comparing content that way?

D: Yeah.

A: Well, I think of content as subject matter.

C: I think content is the generation of ideas, and they generated more ideas in A.

What differences do you notice in the information on the blackboard at the end of the lesson [see Figs. 1–2 and 1–3]?

C: I thought the information was about the same, except that Lesson A gave more examples and Lesson B gave more terms.

A: In Lesson B the teacher's language is used—"punctuation," "predicate," and so forth. So they're given more information there.

B: It *is* more information. She's covered a great deal.

D: Yeah, but do the kids understand it?

B: *I* understood it, but I don't know if a fourth-grader would. She's teaching the structure of the sentences in Lesson B, and I think she should have gone over what subjects and predicates are before.

C: Well the kids might have had another lesson on that.

B: But she should at least review.

A: I'd like to know what the follow-up for each of these lessons will be. Like, in Lesson A, will she tell them more about predicates and subjects the next time?

B: Which group do you think would do better on the worksheet at the end?

D: I think A would.

C: Well, maybe not at the end of this lesson, but probably in later lessons, the A group would be better able to apply the ideas.

ADDITIONAL ANALYSIS

Some of the points raised by the students in the foregoing discussion are valid ones. Some of the doubts and critical feelings about discovery methods voiced here are shared by many classroom teachers. We believe that if people understood the discovery process more fully, many of these doubts would disappear, and the feelings of criticism would be replaced by determination to solve some of the "problems" associated with teaching by discovery.

As we see it, the first step in understanding the discovery method is to distinguish clearly between it and a more direct method of teaching. To that end, we present some analytical comments of our own. These comments are based upon our observations of many lessons of both types, although we only provide illustrations from the two lessons presented earlier in this chapter.

COMPARISON OF LESSON PLANS

Most readers notice that there are more objectives listed in Lesson Plan A than in Lesson Plan B. The additional objectives in A have to

do with development of thinking skills and practice in sentence transformations, or application of the concept being taught. Another difference
is that Lesson A aims at having the children begin to see differences in
sentence types, while Lesson B aims at a more finished product, in that
children should be able to identify sentences of different types.

In summarizing these differences it might be said that Lesson A
deals with a wider variety of skills and knowledge but does not aim at
a complete understanding of the three sentence types in this single lesson.
Lesson B deals with a smaller range of knowledge and aims at a more
rapid understanding of the particular concept in question. The plans are
similar in that they both deal with the same concept.

Most readers notice that the materials used in the two lessons are
basically the same. Both lessons begin with the same twelve sentences on
the board. Both lessons end with the same worksheet.

The materials are not identical, however. Lesson Plan A provides
two more examples of each sentence type at the beginning of the lesson.
Children write additional examples of their own; so, in a sense they are
producing more materials as the lesson progresses.

Basic differences exist in the procedures used in the two lessons. In
Lesson A the teacher *asks* the children how the three sentence types
differ. In Lesson B the teacher *tells* the children how they differ.

Plans for evaluation of learning in the two lessons are similar in
that both utilize the worksheet as evidence of children's understanding
of the concept. Lesson Plan B focuses primarily on whether children are
able to apply the concepts learned in categorizing new sentences. Lesson
Plan A evaluates children's ability to observe the "data" or sample sentences and to apply the concepts by producing sentence transformations
themselves. As would be expected from differences in objectives, Lesson
Plan A seeks to evaluate a wider variety of skills.

COMPARISON OF TEACHER BEHAVIOR

As noted above, the basic difference in teaching behavior is that the
teacher *asks* in Lesson A and *tells* in Lesson B. Most readers are able to
identify some less obvious differences in addition to this.

One difference is that in Lesson A the teacher generally asks children to evaluate each other's responses. The following exchanges are examples of this behavior:

T: Pam, what do you think?
Pam: "Will José mow the lawn?"
T: How many think Pam is right?
(Hands go up.)

T: All right, let's put that down then. . . . Now is there anyone who thinks they know what should go in sentence 5 in this column? Steve?

Steve: "José will mow the lawn."

T: How many think Steve is right?

(*A few hands go up.*)

T: How many think it's something else?

(*More hands go up.*)

In Lesson B the teacher generally indicates whether children's answers are right or wrong. The following exchanges are examples of this behavior:

T: Do you think you know what these are called, John?

John: Answers.

T: No. Bobby?

Bobby: An order.

T: That's one way of saying it.

T: Do you all know what punctuation is?

(*Children nod.*)

T: What is it?

Joe: Periods, commas, and question marks.

T: Right.

Another difference in teaching behavior is that the teacher in Lesson A frequently asks children to *think* about a particular example to see if they can figure out why it fits. She rarely asks them to *state* their reasons for the particular forms of sentences they generate, however. The following exchange is an example of this:

T: I'm going to write down, "Mow the lawn." Steve, you can think about the difference between what you said and what Kim said.

Jean: Oh, I see, I see.

T: Well, we're not going to talk about it right now. We'll give everyone a chance to think about it.

In Lesson B the teacher does ask children to state their reasons for classifying sentences in particular ways, but does not ask them to think about these for any length of time. When reasons do not come easily, the teacher asks leading questions of the children. The following dialogue is an example of this behavior:

T: Tom, what do you think?

Tom: It's a statement.

T: Tell us why you think it's a statement.

Tom: Because it tells you what somebody is going to do.

T: That's another way of telling a statement. You're right. Statements tell us what somebody is doing. Tony, do you have another idea?

Tony: Well, where it has "Go to the movies," that doesn't show the name, so it can't be one of those. And it isn't a question, so it has to be a statement.

Tom: Oh, boy!

T: Tony says it has a name. What is the name?

Tony: "José."

T: And what is that in the sentence?

Several children: Subject.

T: Where is the subject of that sentence?

Several children: Beginning of the sentence.

T: OK. And that's what statements have—subjects at the beginning of the sentence.

One reason for this difference may be the teacher's need to evaluate children's understanding during the course of the lesson. In Lesson A the teacher can accept correct transformations as evidence that children understand some of the basic differences between sentences. In Lesson B correct classification could more easily be the result of guessing, so the teacher seeks further evidence that children understand the reason for the classification.

A third difference in teaching behavior in the two lessons is that the teacher talks much more in Lesson B than in Lesson A, although Lesson B is a shorter lesson. An example of this behavior is found in the following monologue from Lesson B:

T: Now when somebody makes a statement—says something like, "She is washing the dishes"—there are lots of different things you can do. You might make a comment back. You might say something like, "Well it's about time she washed the dishes." Or you might not say anything at all. When somebody makes a statement, sometimes people say something and sometimes they don't. So the reaction to a statement can be different kinds of things. You might have some *action* after a statement. For example, if somebody said, "John finished his homework," you might clap. That's if John didn't finish his homework very often. But the reaction for a statement can be different kinds of things. You don't always answer a statement. You do usually *listen* to a statement.

The longest teacher comment in Lesson A involves giving directions rather than information, as follows:

T: Now we have ten sentences in each column. You did very well filling those in. What I'd like to know now is, can you write some sentences of your own which fit in those columns? You have some papers on your desks. I want you to try to write one sentence to fit in each of the three columns. Write one sentence to go in column 1, one sentence to go in column 2, and one sentence to go in column 3.

A fourth difference in teaching behavior is that the teacher in Lesson A leaves some problems open for later solution. This is most obvious when we compare the handling of the position of the subject in commands. In Lesson B the teacher explains that the subject in a command is not stated. In Lesson A the problem of the subject in a command is left open for further consideration.

This is a difference that disturbed some of the student discussants whose comments you read earlier. We feel that there is a great deal of value in leaving questions open for later consideration, and this matter will be discussed further in later chapters.

To summarize briefly, the differences in teaching behavior that most students and teachers see in comparing these two lessons are:

Lesson A	*Lesson B*
Teacher asks.	Teacher tells.
Teacher has children evaluate each other's responses.	Teacher decides what answers are right or wrong.
Teacher asks children to think, but not to give verbal explanation.	Teacher asks children to give explanations and uses leading questions.
Teacher talks less.	Teacher talks more.
Teacher leaves some problems for later solution.	Teacher leaves no questions open for later solution.

You may have identified other differences in addition to these.

COMPARISON OF CHILDREN'S BEHAVIOR

Most readers will also note differences in the behavior of children in these two lessons. For one thing, children in Lesson A construct or generate sentences of their own, while children in Lesson B categorize sentences written by the teacher. For another thing, the children in Lesson A indicate disagreement with each other on their own initiative. An example of this occurs in the following dialogue:

T: Is there anything else that you can say is the same about all the sentences in column 2?

Danny: They all have capitals at the beginning.

T: That's true. They all do have capitals at the beginning.

Gary: But every sentence has a capital at the beginning.

In Lesson B the children do not take the initiative in disagreeing with each other. They do, however, offer alternative answers after the teacher says an answer is wrong:

T: Who thinks they can find the predicate in the first sentence in column 1? Tony?

Tony: "The movie."

T: That's part of it, but there's more to it than that. Barry?

Barry: "To the movie."

T: Well, there's still a little more. Lon?

Lon: "Is going to the movie."

T: That's right.

Another difference in children's behavior is that the answers in Lesson A tend to be longer than the answers in Lesson B. A brief sampling of children's answers from each lesson reads as follows:

Lesson A

Eric: "Can you tell a funny joke?"

Cynthia: "Will you eat your vegetables?"

Steve: Number 9 in column 1 would be "You will eat your vegetables."

Tammy: They're all questions.

Danny: They all have capitals at the beginning.

Judy: They're using "be" words.

Mike: You mean the "be" words? Well, they're asking a question, and some of them are at the beginning and some of them are in the middle.

Greg: No. They're not telling you what to do, they're telling you what somebody else is doing.

Lesson B

Bobby: An order.

Joe: Periods, commas, and question marks.

Lorelei: Moving.

Tom: If you do something and somebody else does the same thing.

Rachel: "The boy."

Candy: "Hit the ball."

Tommy: "Did" and "finish his homework."

Tom: It's a statement.

Rachel: It tells you what to do.

Class: Yes.

Class: No.

Tony: You.

Karen: At the end.

The differences noted above are all observable differences. Frequently teachers comment upon other differences in children's reactions which are not really observable. Many teachers seem to think that the children in Lesson A are more interested. This is not a difference which is obvious from reading a transcript of a lesson.

Other teachers comment that the children in Lesson A must be more anxious about the lesson because they aren't told what answers are right and at the end of the lesson they can't be sure what they ought to know, or what they ought to think. This is not really an *observable* difference either. The question of the role of anxiety in a discovery lesson is an important one, however. It will be discussed later.

COMPARISON OF CONTENT AND INFORMATION

In studying the blackboard at the end of the two lessons (Figs. 1–2 and 1–3) most teachers and students identify three differences in the content and information dealt with. First they note that more content is covered in Lesson B, or that the children have been presented with a more complete concept. For example, they have heard about the subject/predicate relationship in the three sentence types, while the children in Lesson A have not discussed predicates at all. They have only talked about "be" words, or forms of "be."

Another difference noted is that the children in Lesson A have considered more examples of each sentence type, or have looked at more data. They have about fifteen examples of each sentence type recorded on the blackboard, compared with six examples of each type for Lesson B.

A third difference is that the identifying characteristics of each sentence type are recorded in the children's words in Lesson A. They are recorded in the teacher's words in Lesson B.

SUMMARY

In comparing these two lessons we have noted differences in objectives, procedures, methods of evaluation, teacher behavior, children's behavior, content, and information. We have also noted similarities in content and materials. You may have noted some differences not mentioned here.

What does this cataloging of differences accomplish? The most important result, we feel, is that it leads to an identification of some of the characteristics of discovery lessons. Of course, one example is not enough for us to form a valid generalization. Nevertheless, the authors have taught and observed many discovery lessons and find that most of them have similar characteristics.

DIRECT AND INDIRECT TEACHING

In connection with his study of teaching behavior, Ned Flanders identifies two types of teachers: those who tend to use "direct" influence and those who tend to use "indirect" influence. The behavior characteristic of each type of influence is as follows:[2]

Direct Influence	*Indirect Influence*
1. Expresses or lectures about his own ideas	1. Accepts, clarifies, and supports the ideas of pupils

---

[2] Ned Flanders, "Teacher Influence in the Classroom," in Bellack (1963).

2. Gives direction or orders	2. Praises and encourages
3. Criticizes or deprecates pupil behavior	3. Asks questions to stimulate pupil participation in decision making
4. Justifies his own authority	4. Asks questions to orient pupils to schoolwork

If we view the direct-indirect distinction as a continuum rather than a dichotomy, we might place both Lesson A and Lesson B along that continuum. Lesson A would fall toward the "indirect" end, because the teacher asked for and used children's ideas. Lesson B would fall toward the "direct" end of the continuum because the teacher lectured about her own ideas.

Some of the research on teaching behavior seems to indicate relationships between teaching behavior and student achievement. Of particular interest in relation to use of "indirect" influence are the following findings:[3]

1. When teaching behavior was indirect instead of direct, students more easily developed principles of self-direction and management.
2. Highest achievement is found in classes of teachers who make frequent use of children's ideas.
3. Achievement is superior in classes of teachers who ask questions frequently.
4. When teachers ask vague, unstructured questions as compared to highly specific, structured questions, class achievement is lower.
5. Reacting to students' answers by asking further clarifying questions has been associated with higher achievement.

The inductive discovery lesson of which Lesson A is one example can be viewed as one type of lesson which makes use of indirect teacher influence. We have found it helpful to compare lessons aimed at attainment of particular concepts in terms of direct and indirect influence. The differences between Lesson A and Lesson B are characteristic of differences between concept attainment lessons of the more direct and more indirect type. These lesson types can be viewed as lesson "models," and characterized as in Table 1–1.

[3] These findings are reported by several studies including those of Cogan (1958); Conners and Eisenberg (1966); Fortune (1967); Harris and Serwer (1966); Morrison (1966); Perkins (1951); Soar (1966); Spaulding (1963); and Wallen (1966) (see References at the back of this volume).

TABLE 1–1 LESSON MODELS FOR CONCEPT ATTAINMENT

Direct: Lecture or Prescriptive Lesson	*Indirect: Inductive Discovery Lesson*
Objectives	
1. *Rapid* attainment of a particular concept	1. Development of thinking skills
	2. *Eventual* attainment of a particular concept
Procedures	
1. Use familiar materials.	1. Use familiar materials.
2. Use both examples and nonexamples of concept.*	2. Use both examples and nonexamples of concept.*
3. Define student role as *attaining* the correct concept.	3. Define student role as *searching* or *testing* ideas.
4. Tell students the concept, explain, and give several examples.	4. Give students many examples of the concept and ask them to figure it out.
5. Provide materials for students to apply the concept.	5. Provide materials for students to test their ideas.
6. Tell students if they are right or wrong.	6. Have students evaluate their own ideas.
7. Work for "closure," or to have students feel they have attained the correct concept.	7. Encourage students to reserve judgment, leave some questions open for later solution.
Evaluation	
1. Do students know the concept?	1. Can students modify and revise concept on basis of new evidence?
2. Can they apply the concept in new situations?	2. Can they apply the concept in new situations?

* The importance of nonexamples will be discussed further in Chapter 3.

POINTS TO REMEMBER

1. The most effective teacher is one who uses a *variety* of procedures. No one kind of lesson is good for all purposes.

2. A lesson "model" is only a way of describing reality. Few *real* lessons ever follow a model completely.

3. An "indirect" lesson is *not* unplanned.

chapter 2

Attaining Concepts

One problem that many teachers have in planning and conducting inductive discovery lessons is that they are uncertain as to exactly what "concepts" and "data" are. Concepts can vary from relatively simple ideas to rather complex ones. Basically a concept is a way of organizing or perceiving the information that we receive from the world around us, the "input" to our minds.

A simple concept such as "red" helps us to perceive all colors within a certain portion of the spectrum as being similar. This concept is simple because it deals with only *one* attribute or characteristic of each of the objects we might label as red. The data which children use in arriving at the concept of red will vary, but some typical examples are probably: a red traffic light, a red ball, a red dress, a red flower, a red truck. These objects form one set of data, but unless they are accompanied by another set of data—the sound of the word *red* in connection with each of these objects—it is extremely doubtful that children will learn the concept. Thus data pertinent to even a simple concept can be of more than one type.

An example of a more complex concept, usually called a generalization, would be the statement, "Men are more alike than different," derived from cultural anthropology. This generalization may cause us to attend to particular aspects of man more than to others. If we really believe this generalization, then we will tend to notice and recall instances which demonstrate similarities among men of various races and cultures. The data from which this generalization is formed are other generalizations, such as: all men live in groups; all groups of men use language for the purpose of communication; all groups of men organize themselves into smaller units, like the family. These generalizations were originally formulated from other propositions, such as: Frenchmen speak French; Navajo Indians speak Navajo; Argentinians speak Spanish; etc. These statements in turn were derived from a series of specific facts (data), such as: Pierre is a Frenchman who speaks French; Jacquelyn is a Frenchwoman who speaks French; Jacques is a French boy who speaks French. Again we can see that the data pertinent to the ultimate generalization is of many types. In the complex concept or generalization the "sense data," or the specific facts which are directly observable, are apt to be much further removed from the concept.

Much of the literature on how children and adults learn concepts labels this process "concept formation." Bruner has distinguished between concept formation and "concept attainment," suggesting that the educator is really concerned with the latter:

> Concept formation is essentially the first step en route to attainment. In the case of mushrooms (for example), the formation of the hypothesis that *some* mushrooms are edible and *others* are not is the act of forming a concept. *Attainment* refers to the process of finding predictive defining attributes that distinguish exemplars from nonexemplars of the class one seeks to discriminate.[1]

For Bruner, then, concept formation means the process of deciding that a class or group exists. For example, a few years ago someone noted that some teen-agers differed rather markedly from the typical teen-ager, and coined the term *hippie*. Noting that a group existed, and naming the group, involved a process of concept formation.

Once the term *hippie* was invented, people began to argue over what a "hippie" was. Some thought it was anyone with long hair. Some thought it was anyone who didn't work. Some thought it was anyone who was dirty. Some thought it was anyone who hitchhiked. Those who joined the controversy were involved in a process of concept attainment. They were trying to identify the "criterial attributes," the qualities or characteristics that made one person a hippie and another person a non-hippie.

Today many people have *formed* the concept "hippie," in the sense that they know that such a group is said to exist. But they have not *attained* the concept "hippie," because they cannot come to a general agreement about what exactly characterizes a member of that group.

When Bruner suggests that the educator is not really concerned with concept formation, he means that we seldom try to get children in school to invent new concepts, or to discover new groups or classes whose existence has gone unnoticed before. In most instances when we try to help children in school to develop concepts, we are working with concepts

---

[1] Jerome S. Bruner et al., *A Study of Thinking* (New York: John Wiley & Sons, 1961), p. 22.

or classes which already exist, such as nouns and verbs, or mammals and reptiles. The children in many cases know that such classes exist, or have heard the names of the classes used by parents or other children. They may know that some words are called nouns and others are called verbs. What they do not know, and what we hope to teach them, are the characteristics or attributes which identify a word as a noun or a verb. This involves a process of *concept attainment,* in the sense in which Bruner uses the term. Most teachers will find it helpful to think in terms of concept attainment while using the inductive discovery method with children.

CONCEPT ATTAINMENT EXERCISES

Beginning at the top of page 29 is a series of exercises designed to give the reader some experience with the process of concept attainment. Solving these exercises and analyzing various responses to them should provide some insight into the problems that children face when they are involved in inductive discovery.

Directions: Carefully study the materials provided and answer the questions asked. When you have attempted solutions to all the exercises, you will be asked which concepts were easiest for you to attain and which were hardest. As you work through the problems it may be helpful to consider what makes some more difficult than others. *Do not read the rest of this page now.* When you have finished the exercises A–E, which begin at the top of page 29, then continue reading below.

SOME EXPECTED RESPONSES

Concept A. A glump is any geometric form bounded by a square. The square must contain a figure, but the figure can be an open or closed form.

In arriving at this definition, or an approximation of it, you may have considered one or more of the following possibilities:

a. A glump is any figure containing an open or closed form, or a point, or a line.
b. A glump is any figure bounded by a rectangle.
c. A glump is any figure containing another figure.

These possibilities are usually rejected, one by one, as more data are presented. With each successive indication of which examples are glumps and which are not, more ideas about characteristics of glumps can be tested. As more data are collected, certainty about what a glump is tends to increase. If several readers were to compare their ideas about glumps after item 5, after item 10, and after they had stated the characteristics of a glump, they would probably find much more agreement among their final statements than among their ideas after completing item 5.

Concepts B and E. These concepts are the same. Words are arranged in sequence. The first word contains one letter, the first letter of the alphabet (*a*). The second word begins with the second letter of the alphabet (*b*) and contains two letters. The third word begins with the third letter of the alphabet (*c*) and contains three letters, and so on to the seventh word, which begins with the seventh letter (*g*) and contains seven letters.

Quite probably you were more certain about your correct attainment of concept E than you were about concept B. We would also predict that several readers comparing their responses would find much more agreement in response to concept E than to concept B. The only difference between the two problems as presented in B and E, however, was that more data or more information was given in problem E.

AMOUNTS OF DATA

One factor that has a great deal of influence on concept attainment is the amount of data that the student or problem solver has. As more data are provided, more ideas can be tested. Some will be rejected; some will remain as possibilities.

It is important, however, that additional data contain additional information. For example, suppose the series of items in concept A on page 29 had been:

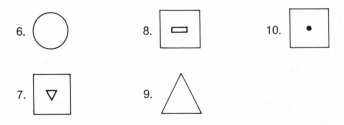

Then you would not have been able to generate many new ideas about possible characteristics of a glump. These items are very similar to items 1–5, so they do not provide much additional information.

Generally speaking, the more data that are provided, the faster

EXERCISES

A. The following items are called *glumps*. Study them carefully.

Now look at the following series of items and indicate for each whether or not it is a glump:

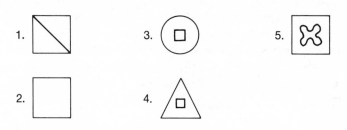

When you have finished, turn to the top of page 31.

EXERCISES

B. Below you are given the beginning and the end of something. You are to fill in the missing parts in the middle.[2]

A, be   gallops

When you have finished, turn to page 31 and do exercise C.

---

students will attain a concept, and the more apt they will be to attain the same concept. The teacher can use this information to control results of a lesson to some extent. If he wants fairly rapid attainment of a concept, and agreement among children on what the concept is, he will provide larger amounts of data. If he wants more gradual attainment of the concept, with some disagreement among children, requiring that each

[2] This problem is similar to one developed by Sir Frederick Bartlett in his book *Thinking: An Experimental and Social Study* (London: George Allen and Unwin, 1958).

child give evidence to support his own generalization, then the teacher will provide smaller amounts of data. In the first case, the teacher will be emphasizing the learning of a concept. In the second case he will be emphasizing the learning of techniques of investigation, such as means of testing a generalization. We shall discuss this point further in a later chapter.

Concept C. This concept involves the organization of numbers in a sequence: 2, 4, 6, 8, 10.

It is probable that you were quite certain that you had attained this concept. It is also probable that many people would agree in their solution of this problem. This is interesting when we compare concept C with concept B. Both concepts give the same amount of data—three items. Both concepts relate to sequence of numbers. Why should there be a difference in your response to these two concepts? We suggest that you list your ideas about this before continuing with the next section.

COMPLEXITY AND CONTEXT

In comparing concepts B and C some of you may have noted that concept B is really more complex. It involves a sequence of numbers *in combination with* a sequence of letters. You may have concluded from this observation that complex concepts (those which involve more than one identifying characteristic) are more difficult to attain than simple concepts. Few would argue with this conclusion.

It is possible that a few of you have again considered concept E and noted that with additional data you were able to attain the more complex concept. In E you had five items of data, while in C you had three items. This may suggest to you that a more complex concept such as B requires more data for solution, as in exercise E, than does a simple concept such as C. This is an interesting possibility, and you may wish to devise some way of testing it.

Another difference between concepts B and C may also be noted. In concept C the type of data used is generally found in a context similar to that of the concept. That is, numbers are frequently found in sequence. Both the idea of number and the idea of sequence are commonly associated in the context of mathematics. In concept C the data suggests the context of mathematics, and the concept to be attained is one appropriate to this context.

In concept B the data (words) suggest the context of language. Language is usually associated with *meaningful* sequences. Many of you undoubtedly responded to concept B by trying to construct sentences, because the use of words as data channeled your thinking toward concepts appropriate to the context of language.

EXERCISES

A. *(cont.)* You were correct if you identified items 1 and 5 as glumps. Items 2, 3, and 4 are not glumps.

Indicate whether or not each of the following items is a glump.

 6. 8. 10.

 7. 9.

When you have finished, turn to the top of page 33.

EXERCISES

C. Below you are given the beginning and end of something. You must fill in the missing parts in the middle.

2, 4   10

When you have finished, turn to page 33 and do exercise D.

It is apparent that the context within which the problem solver searches for possible solutions can affect concept attainment. If no context is provided by the directions, then the problem solver must provide his own context or area of search for possible defining criteria. Sometimes the data will be helpful in suggesting an appropriate context, as in concept C. Sometimes the data will be misleading in this regard, as in concept B.

CONVERGENT AND DIVERGENT THINKING

By providing a context for search the teacher can encourage convergent thinking. According to Mary Jane Aschner, convergent thinking involves

thought processes that are both analytical and integrated, and that operate within a closely structured framework. Nevertheless, they are productive thought processes. . . . Solutions to problems . . . are reached by reasoning based on given and/or remembered data. Something more is involved than mere retrieval of remembered material; something is produced, though clearly not "invented" in any creative sense.[3]

To put it another way, if several people are provided with the same problem to solve and they all come up with the same solution, they are probably involved in convergent thinking. The information that they have to work with has channeled their thinking in particular ways, and thus their ideas converge. Many of the questions that children are asked in school tend to encourage convergent thinking because they are highly structured questions.

In concept D the question you were asked was not very structured, but it would be possible to encourage more convergent thinking, or more similarity of response, by making the question or directions more structured. For example, we might consider the effect of the following change in directions for concept D. Without looking back to your earlier response, organize the following items into groups of things which have a similar function in society:

man	saucer	crib	horse
baby	dog	train	chair
cup	car	cat	plate
bottle	woman	table	rattle

We would predict that most readers will respond to these changed directions by forming the following groups:

cup, saucer, plate, bottle—used for eating
car, train—used for transportation
crib, table, chair—used for furniture
dog, cat, horse—used as pets
rattle—used as toy
man, woman, baby—function as a family or group in society

Those who do not have these exact groups probably have some organization that approximates them fairly closely. The context or area of possible appropriate ideas was narrowed by adding the notion of "function in society" to the directions. As a result, more convergent thinking was used.

---

[3] Mary Jane Aschner, "The Analysis of Verbal Interaction in the Classroom," in Bellack (1963).

EXERCISES

A. *(cont.)* If you identified items 6, 8, and 10 as glumps, you were correct. Items 7 and 9 are not glumps.

What are the defining characteristics of a glump?

When you have completed your definition, turn back to page 29 and begin work on exercise B.

EXERCISES

D. Organize the following items into groups of things that are similar or that belong together. You may have as many groups as you like. An item can only be included in *one* group.

man	saucer	crib	horse
baby	dog	train	chair
cup	car	cat	plate
bottle	woman	table	rattle

When you have completed your groups, do exercise E below.

E. Below you are given the beginning and the end of something. You must fill in the missing parts in the middle.

A, be, can, drum   gallops

QUESTIONS TO CONSIDER

1. Which of the preceding concepts (A–E) are you most sure of—that is, most certain that you have attained the correct concept?
2. Which concept are you least sure of?
3. Why are you more sure of one than another?
4. Which of the preceding concepts was presented in the most "direct" manner—that is, using procedures most similar to the direct or prescriptive lesson. Which concept was presented in the least direct manner?

In contrast, there are a large number of typical responses to concept D as originally presented. Some of these are:

1. baby, bottle, crib, rattle
    cup, saucer, plate
    table, chair
    dog, cat, horse
    car, train
    man, woman

2. *Paired objects*

    baby and bottle
    man and woman
    cup and saucer
    table and chair
    dog and cat

    Unpaired objects

    crib
    rattle
    plate
    horse
    car
    train

3. *Living*

    man
    woman
    baby
    cat
    dog
    horse

    Nonliving

table	crib
chair	rattle
cup	car
saucer	train
plate	bottle

4. | *In house* | *Outside* | *Go in and out* |
    |---|---|---|
    | table | car | man |
    | chair | train | woman |
    | crib | horse | baby |
    | cup | | cat |
    | saucer | | dog |
    | plate | | |
    | rattle | | |
    | bottle | | |

5. | *Moving things* | *Stationary things* |
    |---|---|
    | man | cup |
    | woman | saucer |
    | baby | plate |
    | car | table |
    | train | chair |
    | cat | crib |
    | dog | bottle |
    | horse | rattle |

6. *3-letter words*

man
cup
dog
cat
car

4-letter words

baby
crib

5-letter words

woman
train
table
horse
chair
plate

6-letter words

bottle
saucer
rattle

7. *Alphabetical groupings*
baby, bottle
cat, car, chair, crib, cup
dog
horse
man
plate
rattle
saucer
table, train
woman

Other possible arrangements also exist, of course, and all are appropriate kinds of responses to concept D as originally stated. The fact that no context was provided encouraged *divergent* responses to this problem.

Divergent thinking is defined as

performance . . . indicative of initiative, spontaneity, ideational fluency, originality and ingenuity, penetration and flexibility in problem solving, and the like. . . . Problems and questions which invite divergent thinking provide for its operation within a definite framework, but one which is "data-poor" in such a way as to cast the person upon his own initiative and his own resources. There must be room and opportunity to generate many and varied ideas, associations, and conclusions.[4]

4 Aschner, "Analysis of Verbal Interaction," p. 65.

To put it another way, if several people are provided with the same problem to solve and they all come up with different solutions, they are probably involved in divergent thinking: the information that they have to work with does not direct their thinking very closely, so they draw upon their own background, interests, and knowledge to structure the problem for them, and their ideas tend to diverge.

Analysis of typical responses to the foregoing concepts seems to suggest that the teacher can affect children's use of convergent and divergent thinking by controlling the factor of context in concept attainment. The more closed the context (or the more structured the directions), the more convergent the thinking, and the more similar the concepts suggested as solutions. The more open the context, the more divergent the thinking, and the more variety in the concepts suggested as solutions.

Of the concepts worked with so far, most readers seem to feel that concept A is the most structured, or the most "direct," and that concept D is the least structured, or least direct.

FACTORS INFLUENCING CONCEPT ATTAINMENT

On the basis of responses to five concept attainment exercises we have seen that certain factors can have favorable or unfavorable effects on our ability to attain concepts. The factors we have noted so far are amount of data, complexity of concept, and context provided for search. By manipulating these factors the teacher can affect the speed of concept attainment and the amount of agreement on the concept.

As you work through the next set of concept attainment exercises, try to think of other factors which may be influencing your responses.

ADDITIONAL CONCEPT ATTAINMENT EXERCISES

F. A generalization from the field of child development is that sex roles are learned through imitation: girls imitate the female role; boys imitate the male role; girls and boys engage in different types of play.

The pictures in Fig. 2–1 are numbered. Some provide evidence to support this generalization, and some do not. Complete the statements below with the appropriate numbers:

This generalization is supported by pictures numbered 1, 2, . . .
This generalization is *not* supported by pictures numbered 3, 4, . . .

1

2

3

Fig. 2–1

37

4

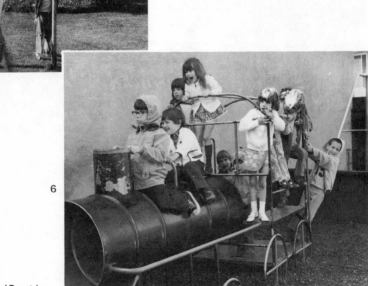

5

6

Fig. 2–1 (Cont.)

7

8

9

Fig. 2–1 (Cont.)

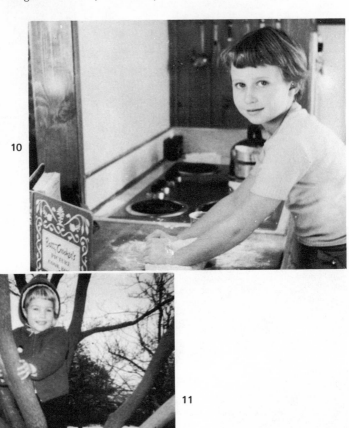

Fig. 2–1 (Cont.)

G. In Fig. 2–2, compare the photographs in group A with those in group B. Answer the following questions:

1. How are the pictures in group A similar to those in group B?
2. How are the pictures in group A different from those in group B?
3. What concept is illustrated by group A?

Group A

Fig. 2–2

Group B

Fig. 2–2 (Cont.)

H. Figure 2–3 is a picture of several common objects. Each item is labeled "yes" if it is an example of the concept. It is labeled "no" if it is not an example of the concept. What is the concept?

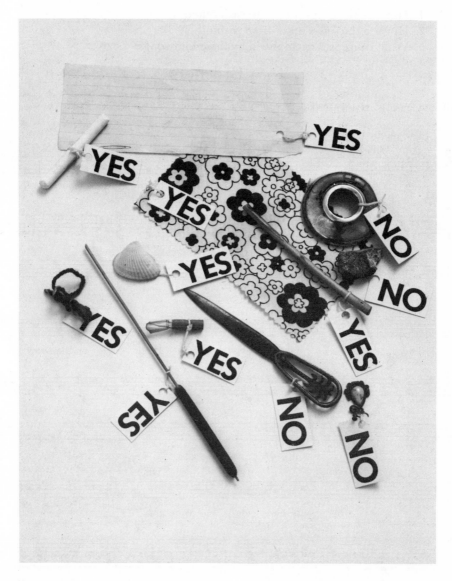

Fig. 2–3

I. Figure 2–4 shows four songs: "Two Brothers," "When Johnny Comes Marching Home," "Over There," and "Around Her Neck She Wore a Yellow Ribbon." Compare the songs. Answer the following questions:

1. How are the songs similar to each other?
2. How do the songs differ from each other?
3. What concept is exemplified by these four songs?

Two Brothers

Words and music by Irving Gordon

Fig. 2–4a

TWO BROTHERS (Cont.)

POST-WAR SONGS

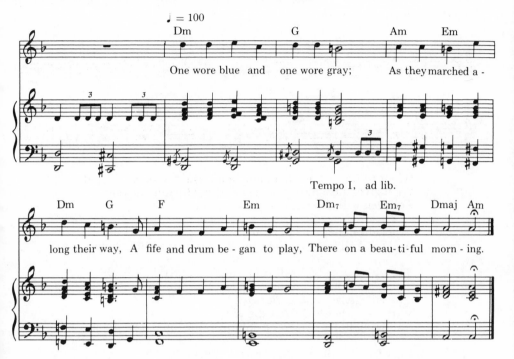

2. One was gentle, one was kind,
   One was gentle, one was kind,
   One came home, one stayed behind;
   A cannon ball don't pay no mind,
   A cannon ball don't pay no mind,
   Though you're gentle or you're kind,
   It don't think of the folks behind,
   There on a beautiful morning.

3. Two girls waitin' by the railroad track,
   Two girls waitin' by the railroad track,
   For their darlin's to come back;
   One wore blue and one wore black,
   One wore blue and one wore black,
   Waitin' by the railroad track,
   For their darlin's to come back,
   There on a beautiful morning.

Fig. 2–4a (Cont.)

Reprinted from *Songs of the Civil War,* edited by Irwin Silber. (New York: Columbia University Press, 1960.) Piano arrangement by Jerry Silverman. Words and music copyright 1951 by Shapiro, Bernstein & Co., Inc., 666 Fifth Ave., New York, N.Y. 10019. Used by permission.

WHEN JOHNNY COMES MARCHING HOME

Now he is a hero, and his song belongs to all the wars. Paul S. Gilmore, the fa-mous bandmaster, wrote this one.

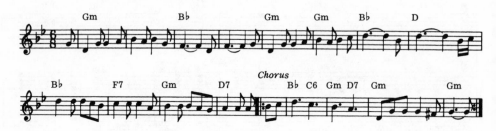

When Johnny comes marching home again, Hurrah, hurrah!
We'll give him a hearty welcome then, Hurrah, hurrah!
The men will cheer, the boys will shout,

The ladies, they will all turn out,
And we'll all feel gay when Johnny comes marching home.

The old church bell will peal with joy, Hurrah, hurrah!
To welcome home our darling boy, Hurrah, hurrah!
The village lads and lassies say,
With roses they will strew the way,
And we'll all feel gay when Johnny comes marching home.

Get ready for the jubilee, Hurrah, hurrah!
We'll give the hero three times three, Hurrah, hurrah!
The laurel wreath is ready now
To place upon his loyal brow;
And we'll all feel gay when Johnny comes marching home.

Fig. 2–4b

OVER THERE

In World War I, George M. Cohan's song hit did everything that a composer born on the Fourth of July could wish, but not everyone whistling his tune caught the pun in the first notes of the chorus, which are those of the whippoorwill—that is, "Beat Kaiser Bill." Copyright 1917 (renewed) by Leo Feist, Inc., New York. Used by permission.

Over there, over there,
Send the word, send the word over there
That the Yanks are coming, the Yanks are
      coming,
The drums rum-tumming everywhere.

So prepare, say a pray'r,
Send the word, send the word to beware—
We'll be over, we're coming over,
And we won't come back till it's over
      over there.

Fig. 2–4c

Reprinted from *Songs That Changed the World,* edited by Wanda Willson Whitman. (New York: Crown Publishers, 1969.) Words and music by George M. Cohan, copyright 1917, renewed 1945, by Leo Feist, Inc. Used by permission.

AROUND HER NECK SHE WORE A YELLOW RIBBON

A genuine folk song of undetermined origin, this one was revived for World War I. The original purple ribbon was changed to yellow for the cavalry, which retained its dash in that war although saber charges were over.

Around her neck she wore a yellow ribbon,
She wore it in December and in the month of May,
And if you asked her why the decoration,
She said 'twas for her lover who was far, far away.

Far away, far away—she wore it for a soldier who was far, far away.

Above a grave she scattered yellow flowers,
She brought them in December and in the month of May.
And if you asked her why she came to bring them,
She said 'twas for a soldier who was six feet away.

Fig. 2–4d

AN ANALYSIS OF YOUR OWN THINKING

The last four concept attainment exercises may be responded to in different ways by different people. We suggest that you try to analyze your own responses, and then compare them to those of others in your class or study group. A discussion of this nature generally leads to many insights regarding the factors that influence most people's thinking.

In the chapter that follows we shall present some of the insights developed by other groups who have worked through these same four exercises. You can compare your own ideas to theirs and ours.

You may find the following questions useful in guiding your analysis and discussion:

1. Which of the last four exercises (F–I) was most difficult for you? What do you think made it difficult?
2. Which of the last four exercises was easiest for you? What do you think made it easy?
3. Identify as many factors as you can that affected your concept attainment in exercises F through I.
4. On which of the four concepts do you predict most people will agree? On which will there be the most disagreement? Why?

chapter **3**

Factors Affecting
Discovery

Concept attainment is not an easy task. But most of us find it a rewarding one when we can be fairly certain that we have arrived at a
good answer to the problem. Some of the concepts in the foregoing
chapter were easier to attain than others, and deliberately so. Your
awareness of this is an important first step in improving your techniques
for helping children in the discovery process.

In some cases you might have felt rather uncomfortable or anxious
about not knowing whether your concept was "right." In other cases
you might have become frustrated at not finding a solution, and decided
to quit working on the problem. As teachers we want to provide children
with learning situations which will either avoid these problems or else
show children how to deal with them when they are unavoidable. The
crucial instructional question, of course, is how to do this. As we consider
some further factors which influence the discovery process, we shall try to
help you answer that question. The discussion which follows deals with
these factors of influence in relation to the set of concept attainment
exercises (F–I) presented at the end of Chapter 2.

Exercise F. The pictures in Fig. 2–1 which support the generalization in exercise F are 1, 2, 7, and 10. The pictures which do not support
the generalization are 3, 4, 5, 6, 8, 9, and 11.

We predict that you found exercise F the easiest of exercises F–I.
Most people do, because the generalization is already stated. This provides you with more security or certainty. The presentation is quite
direct. This is also the generalization on which there is usually the most
agreement. Most people agree as to which pictures support the generalization.

Some people dealing with this generalization have noted that some of the data is ambiguous. In some of the pictures it is difficult to tell whether the child is a boy or a girl. This points up the fact that data to be used for development of a convergent concept should be very clear, not open to a variety of interpretations.

Another factor which may make this generalization difficult is hostility to the concept of sex roles. Influenced by the women's liberation movement some persons are too annoyed with the generalization to be able to examine the data objectively. Over the five years that we have been using this particular task with prospective teachers, we have noted a marked increase in the difficulty it presents to female students.

Of course, the generalization as stated has several serious flaws. Sex roles are becoming less and less differentiated in our society.

It is important for us as teachers to consider the purpose to be served by an exercise of this type. As it stands, the exercise encourages application of the generalization to particular situations. Presumably this leads to better understanding of the generalization.

Viewed from another perspective, this exercise focuses on developing skill in a technique of investigation rather than on developing knowledge of a particular concept. The reader is engaged in examining the available evidence to determine how much support there is for the generalization. This is an important part of the discovery process, and one that children must learn how to handle.

Anxiety about whether or not a concept is "right" can be allayed somewhat by teaching children to test their own concepts. We test concepts or generalizations by checking them against new data or new examples of reality. Sometimes the concept or generalization "passes" the test: it fits the new data as well as the original data.

Frequently, as with exercise F, we find that the concept or generalization does not seem to be supported by all new data or evidence. Do we ignore the evidence in such a case? Hopefully not. Do we throw the concept out and start all over? Not usually. We find it more efficient to modify or revise the generalization so that it encompasses both sets of data.

Suppose that you were asked to revise the generalization stated in exercise F in order to make it fit the contradictory evidence. You might say:

Sex roles are learned through imitation. *Young children* tend to imitate adults and older children of *both sexes*. *Older children* identify with those of the *same sex*. Older girls tend to imitate the female role. Older boys tend to imitate the male role. Girls and boys engage in different types of play.

It might eventually be desirable to move from this restatement to one which says:

Sex roles in our society are changing. The roles of girls and boys and men and women are becoming less differentiated.

To reach this revision, additional data would of course be required. This might take the form of photographs from the 1930s compared with photographs from the 1970s. But there are many other types of data that could be used for the same purpose.

Children's anxiety about attaining the "right" concept can be reduced considerably if the teacher plans some lessons dealing with the modification of generalizations. Once children see that concepts can be tested and "corrected" or modified, then getting the "right" answer the first time becomes less important.

Exercise G. The pictures in group A of Fig. 2–2 illustrate the anthropological-sociological concept of the "extended family." The extended family includes grandparents or aunts and uncles in addition to the parents and children. Group B shows examples of the "nuclear family," which consists only of parents and children.

Most readers seem to find this concept easier than concepts H and I. You will note that not very much data are presented. There are only six photographs. Factors other than the amount of data must be affecting attainment of this concept.

One factor you may have noted is that of context. The data are closely related to the context, in that the groups are readily identified as families. This probably started you thinking along particular lines.

Another factor you may have mentioned is the organization of data. You were told which data illustrated the concept. The pictures which illustrated the concept were all together. This tended to improve your observation of the data by making it more concentrated. In effect, your observation was structured by the organization of the data.

Readers with some background in anthropology or sociology probably found this concept easier than did readers not well versed in this subject area. We have found that students not already familiar with the concept of the extended family analyze more aspects of the pictures. They observe that there is more variety of dress depicted in the photographs in group A, for example. Many note that the number of people in each photograph varies quite a bit in group B (from 2 to 9 in a group), while the numbers of people shown in the photographs in group A are all of moderate size. Their statement of the concept usually includes this information.

Students who are familiar with the concept tend to ignore the physical differences among the groups pictured. This fact can be explained in terms of our earlier definition of a concept: a way of organizing or perceiving information coming in from the world around us. The concepts that we have can limit our perceptions in some cases and extend our perceptions in others. In this particular case, having a prior knowledge of the concept of the extended family seems to limit what is observed in the pictures.

Exercise H. The items labeled "yes" in Fig. 2–3 are all materials which were at one time living. They can be called "organic materials."

You may have felt this was the most difficult of the four concepts (F–I). Many people do. They give various reasons for this difficulty.

The organization of the data causes problems for some people. There is a reasonable amount of data, and while each item is labeled to indicate whether it is an example or a "nonexample" of the concept, the data are randomly organized on the page. This means that the observer must keep jumping around from one spot to another to study the data, and many people find this confusing. Organizing all the examples together in one place and all the nonexamples together in another place seems to make concept attainment easier for many people.

Lack of knowledge about the data causes problems for many people. These items are all familiar objects, but some people do not know the origin of some of these objects. The chalk is a particularly good example. You may have had to look up "chalk" in the dictionary to find out whether it is an organic or inorganic material. Concept attainment is usually easier if the materials are familiar and the important characteristics are already known to the observer.

The presentation of the data in this case was not particularly helpful to the process of concept attainment, either. You were given a picture of several objects. The characteristics of those objects which are most important to attainment of the concept (Bruner calls these the "criterial attributes"[1]) were not really observable. Looking at a picture of a piece of paper does not show you that the paper was made from wood pulp. The directions gave no suggestions about what to consider in trying to find similarities among the "yes" items, so the context was fairly open. All of these factors made this concept more difficult to attain.

A divergent response which a few people have made to concept H is that the "yes" items are all in the form of a straight line, or else contain straight lines in their structure or design. This is an accurate statement, and is based on characteristics of the objects that are readily observable.

The teacher who wants to help children be successful at attaining concepts will make an effort to have the presentation of data appropriate to the characteristics to be observed. For example, if you want children to distinguish between flexible and nonflexible materials, it is more ap-

---

[1] Jerome S. Bruner et al., *A Study of Thinking* (New York: John Wiley & Sons, 1961), p. 26.

propriate to give them items to *handle* than to present pictures of those items. In holding and moving and bending a piece of wire, a toothpick, a rubber band, and a pencil, children will observe the presence or absence of an attribute such as flexibility much more readily than they will in looking at a picture of these items.

In the case of concept H, the directions could have read: "What similarities do you see among the 'yes' items? Consider such characteristics as use and origin in trying to find relationships." This change in presentation of the data would provide a more structured context for search and would tend to increase both ease of concept attainment and certainty of the concept after completing the problem.

Exercise I. The four songs in Fig. 2–4 illustrate the concept that war evokes different kinds of emotional reactions, particularly sadness and patriotic fervor.

Many other statements can be made about these songs. This concept is considered the most difficult by many people. In addition it provokes the most divergent responses of the four concepts. Some of the varied responses include:

These songs illustrate the sex-role differences in wartime. Women stay home, worry, keep up the home front, and greet the men on their return. Only men go away and fight.

War always involves separation of families or loved ones. Sometimes they are reunited and sometimes they are not.

Wars may be fought at different times in history (e.g., the Civil War and World War I), but the emotions people feel are usually the same.

People cannot view war objectively. Leaders try to stir up feelings of patriotism to get people to support wars. But really wars make people unhappy.

Music can show different moods or emotions by changing the tempo from fast to slow and by changing the mode from major to minor.

You may have stated a concept different from any of these. The concepts attained are influenced by a number of factors. Some of our students have noted that one factor which affects concept attainment in this exercise is the complexity of the data. There are so many things to think about in relation to each song. The lyrics of each contain a number of different ideas. The music also contains a number of different aspects, such as rhythm, tempo, key, and melodic pattern. Other characteristics are the period when the song was first popular and the composer of the song.

With such a variety of things to select from in looking for relationships among the data, the problem solver is usually guided by his own background and knowledge. People with strong musical backgrounds may focus on the music. People with strong historical backgrounds may focus on the different wars. People with strong backgrounds in sociology may focus on different sex roles.

Some students have noted that their attitudes about war also affect concept attainment in this exercise. You can see that some of the concepts stated above are more "objective" than others. Data which have strong emotional content can interfere with concept attainment, or channel observation in certain directions.

The organization of data is another factor of importance in this exercise. All four songs were illustrative of the concept. No "nonexamples" were presented. Nonexamples function to set up limits. They give the problem solver clues about what the concept is *not*. In this way a few nonexamples can add a great deal of information to the data. The lack of nonexamples in this exercise serves to increase the number of divergent responses, since few limits are placed upon possible appropriate concepts.

Another factor is the form of presentation of data. If the songs are presented to you on a tape, then you have to rely on what you hear and on what you recall. This makes comparison of the data more difficult and tends to focus attention on the *sounds*, such as tempo and mood of the music. If the songs are presented to you in written form, you have more time to study the data. This makes comparison easier and tends to focus attention on the meaning of the words.

FACTORS INFLUENCING CONCEPT ATTAINMENT

We have found that students who attempt these concept attainment exercises are usually able to identify a number of the factors that have affected them in the process of "discovery." You may have listed some of the factors discussed in the foregoing pages in your analysis of your own thinking. Perhaps you listed some other factors that we have not mentioned here.

We have found it useful to organize the factors which influence concept attainment, and particularly that form of concept attainment known as "inductive discovery," into four general types. These are:

1. Factors related to the data
2. Factors related to the context or area of search

3. Factors related to the individual—to the person involved in the concept attainment problem
4. Factors related to the immediate environment (e.g., the classroom)

Examples of the first three types of factors have already been discussed, but it may be helpful to summarize them here. Factors influencing inductive discovery that are related to the data include the amount of data, the organization of data, and the complexity of data. Generally speaking, as more data are accumulated, the concept becomes easier to attain, and the concepts that are attained tend to be more convergent or more similar to each other. As data are more highly organized—e.g., divided into groups of examples and nonexamples rather than randomly placed—observation tends to be more productive, and concepts are more easily attained. As data become more complex, concepts that are formulated tend to be more divergent.

Factors of influence related to the context include the amount of limitation given to the area of search for possible concepts, the suggested methods of observation, and the normal associations between the data and the concept or other concepts. To the extent that the directions given to the problem solver limit the area of search for possible concepts, the concepts attained will tend to be more convergent. Conversely, to the extent that the directions are more open, the concepts attained will tend to be more divergent. Directions given concerning methods of observing the data—e.g., handling concrete materials or substituting words in sentences—will tend to direct attention to particular characteristics of the data. Highly structured directions tend to yield highly convergent responses, and unstructured directions to yield divergent responses. If the data are normally associated in a similar context with the concept to be attained, then attainment of the concept will be easier. If the data are normally associated with *other* concepts, then attainment of the particular concept will be more difficult (e.g., words in numerical sequence rather than more literally meaningful sequences).

Factors related to the individual problem solver also influence inductive discovery. These factors include the background of knowledge, the attitudes, and the cognitive ability of the problem solver. Knowledge of or familiarity with the data tends to make concept attainment easier. Knowledge of the subject matter field (general context) can also make concept attainment easier. The learner's attitudes can interfere with objective observation of data and lead to errors in concept attainment. His attitudes also affect his willingness to suffer the "anxiety" of not knowing whether he has attained the correct concept, and his willingness to persevere in trying to solve a difficult problem. The cognitive ability of the learner also affects his ability to attain concepts. If, for example, he does not yet have the logical ability to classify, he will have difficulty attaining concepts through inductive discovery.

These factors interact, and many of them can be controlled to some extent by the teacher. This means that the teacher can plan inductive discovery lessons aimed chiefly at acquiring knowledge, or rapid attainment of a particular concept, with most children arriving at a similar concept. Alternatively, he can plan inductive discovery lessons aimed chiefly at learning techniques of investigation or *eventual* attainment of a concept, with initial production and testing of a number of different concepts by different children. These two different types of lesson could be diagramed as in Table 3–1.

TABLE 3–1 ARRANGEMENT OF FACTORS OF INFLUENCE IN CONTROLLING
INDUCTIVE DISCOVERY

	Major Objective of Lesson	
Factor	*Acquiring Knowledge*	*Learning Techniques of Investigation*
Data	Provide extra amounts of data.	Provide limited amounts of data.
	Organize data for children.	Let children organize data for themselves.
	Use simple data.	Use complex data.
Context	Limit the area of search for concept.	Extend the area of search for concept, or leave open.
	Limit method of observation to be used.	Leave method of observation open to choice.
Individual	Use materials familiar to learner.	Use some materials that are unfamiliar to learner.

Table 3–1 indicates some of the ways in which the teacher can control factors related to inductive discovery in order to move lessons in particular directions. The teacher cannot *control* factors related to the individual, but he can arrange other factors to fit individual differences. For example, if one child is a slower thinker than another, he can be provided with more data to give him additional help in attaining a concept.

Factors related to the immediate environment that affect inductive discovery—e.g., classroom atmosphere—will be discussed in Part II.

Self-Evaluation of Learning

The first three chapters have dealt with the differences between discovery lessons and prescriptive lessons, and have suggested some of the ways in which various uses of materials may affect the discovery process. You may find it useful to test your own understanding of these ideas by completing the exercise which follows.

Directions: Figure 3–1 is an example of curriculum materials produced by the Education Development Center[1] for use with children in

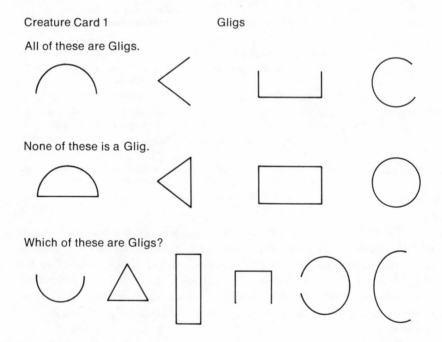

Creature Card 1   Gligs

All of these are Gligs.

None of these is a Glig.

Which of these are Gligs?

Fig. 3–1

[1] Reprinted from the Elementary Science Study Unit, *Attribute Games and Problems*, published by the Webster Division, McGraw-Hill Book Company, copyright 1968 by Education Development Center.

the intermediate grades. Study the sample material. Then answer the questions in the test that follows. Check your answers against the answer sheet on page 236.

TEST ON CONCEPT ATTAINMENT MATERIALS (GLIGS)

OBJECTIVES

1. Reader will classify a given concept attainment exercise as to type of thinking required
2. Reader will appraise the effectiveness of a given concept attainment exercise in regard to amount of data and organization of data
3. Reader will identify the type of teaching model being used in a given concept attainment exercise

CRITERION MEASURE

Upon completion of the concept attainment tasks, the three chapters, and group discussion, the reader should be able to answer 8 of the following 10 questions correctly about any given concept attainment exercise.

Directions: Identify each statement as *true* or *false*. If the statement is false, rewrite the underlined portion to make it true.

_____ 1. This concept attainment exercise requires the student to use inductive thinking.

_____ 2. This concept attainment exercise requires the student to use deductive thinking.

_____ 3. This concept attainment exercise encourages the student to use divergent thinking.

_____ 4. In this exercise inductive, divergent thinking is followed by deductive thinking.

_____ 5. There is a sufficient amount of data for rapid concept attainment.

_____ 6. The presentation includes both examples and nonexamples of the concept.

_____ 7. The data are organized to promote attainment of a variety of possible concepts.

_____ 8. There is no irrelevant data presented to confuse the student.

_____ 9. This concept attainment exercise is organized for a <u>direct</u> teaching style.

_____10. This concept attainment exercise is appropriate for <u>individualized instruction only</u>.

PART II

A CHALLENGE
TO UNDERSTAND THE
TEACHING PROCESS

Teaching by discovery is not an easy task. It takes longer for children to form a generalization on their own than it does for them to learn one that is presented to them prescriptively. It also takes more data. This means that the teacher must work harder to teach a successful discovery lesson.

Some teachers may ask: "Then why bother? Why not use the easier method and teach important concepts by more direct procedures?" In this section we shall explore with you some of the reasons why it is crucial for elementary school children to learn by discovery. There are important attitudinal ends and cognitive skills which children can attain in no other way.

The difficulties of teaching by discovery can be mastered with a little effort. To aid the reader in that effort some basic pedagogical principles for teaching by discovery will be explained and illustrated. These principles can guide the teacher in planning discovery lessons and in making interactive classroom decisions.

Chapters 4, 5, and 6 are designed to present (in a fairly direct manner) a rationale for use of discovery methods and an explanation of the effectiveness of certain teaching procedures common to the discovery format.

4

Ends and Discovery Teaching

Over the last sixty years much has been written about the ends or aims of public and private schools. Much of this discussion has been acrimonious and of little value. Much of it has been very useful, though often ignored by teachers. Attempts have been made to categorize ends, to make them operational, to test them, and to state them clearly, and some attempts have been made to ignore them.

In the political arena the debate still rages over everything from sex education to the teaching of reading, but it is not our intent to enter such controversy here. We must, nevertheless, try to deal with the issue of ends in some intelligent fashion and to relate our discussion to discovery teaching. We shall, therefore, try in this chapter to explicate a few key notions regarding ends and discovery teaching.

Our own view is that one must be clear as to one's ends before venturing into curriculum writing and discussions of how to teach. This necessity extends into the actual process of teaching. A classroom without a teacher who has a clear-cut conception of what he is trying to accomplish is rudderless. Ends give direction to a classroom. Children who sense that the teacher knows where he is going and, consequently, where they are going, feel more secure and act with more purpose. Without this sense of purpose little learning takes place.

But it is not sufficient to say that we wish to teach children to add and thereby set out a set of ends that are purely knowledge ends. It gains us little to teach children to handle mathematics if at the same time we inadvertently teach them to hate mathematics. (We do this in mathematics quite often with girls.) We teach millions of children to read, but many of them use that skill very rarely when they reach adulthood.

It would seem to follow from this and other evidence that historically we have taught many youngsters many things in the area of knowledge and at the same time have taught them not to value what they have learned or not to apply what they have learned. The ideas they have learned are, to use Whitehead's term, inert. The values they have learned are antiknowledge and antithinking.

Krathwohl, Bloom, and Masia note three domains or areas of educational ends—the sensorimotor, the cognitive, and the affective (emotional)—and suggest that each domain is arranged in a hierarchy moving from lower levels to more complex levels.[1] Each higher level incorporates the lower level in its organization. In the cognitive domain the levels are knowledge, comprehension, application, analysis, synthesis, and evaluation. The levels of the affective domain are receiving, responding, valuing, organization, and characterization by a value (or value complex). It occurs to us and to many others that while the lower value levels are sufficient to attain many knowledge ends, any success at the higher cognitive levels calls for involvement at the higher affective levels. Surely the pursuit of knowledge and skills in the academic disciplines requires a high degree of valuing these knowledges and skills, as well as a high degree of commitment in order to sustain the pursuit.

But those who pursue a course of scholarship for any length of time do not suddenly wake up one day and say, "I want to be a scholar." Commitment to learning, love of learning, valuing learning as something positive and worth doing is learned. This value is learned because one has succeeded in gaining knowledge in the past under pleasant conditions. Knowledge is valued because in the process of learning, one's self-concept was enhanced, one's belief in oneself was reinforced. Rewards, public and private, were the result of learning to read, to write, to figure, to think, to construct a hypothesis. Commitment to learning is developed by individuals because someplace along the line learning history, mathematics, or what-have-you became important to the individual. It was learned or pursued not because it pleased others, or was rewarded by others, or was demanded by others, but because it was pleasing, rewarding, and demanding to the individual. When this point is reached, diplomas are a by-product and not an end.

The consequence of what we are saying is that to teach a child to become a student is to offer him a set of conditions that not only lead to gaining knowledge, but also to valuing knowledge and its pursuit. This doesn't mean, as some would have it, a classroom without anxiety, conflict, or frustration. It does mean that the anxiety, conflict, and frus-

---

[1] David R. Krathwohl, Benjamin S. Bloom, Bertram B. Masia, *Taxonomy of Educational Objectives* (New York: David McKay Company, 1964).

tration between *individuals* is reduced, if not eliminated. The anxiety, conflict, and frustration is in the relationship between the child and the reality he is examining, or the child and the truth he is pursuing at the moment.

The young child may set out to learn to read, or to handle numbers, because the teacher has posed the problem. He continues to learn because now that it has been presented the *child* is curious and determines to solve the problem.

The anxiety of gaining closure, the frustration of a faulty hypothesis and inadequate comprehension, and the conflict inside oneself and between one's pet views and the reality of the problem are trying enough for the mature scholar, let alone a young child. But it is not these anxieties, frustrations, and conflicts that lead a child to hate school or to run from a problematic situation. It's the anxiety of needing to find an answer for the teacher in too little time. It's the frustration of finding a truth and then finding out that your truth is not acceptable because it isn't the truth the teacher had in mind. It's the constant conflict of wanting to pursue one subject or topic and the teacher insisting you pursue another. It's the frustration of studying hard to learn one set of facts and being tested on another set, or being told a year later that in this class we believe something else. It's the anxiety of competition with peers not to gain truth but to gain praise, to gain marks, to gain a little peace and quiet. It's the frustration of being repeatedly told you're wrong when you are in a situation where no one could figure out what is right from the information given. It's the conflict that arises when you know the system says one thing to you and does the opposite. The teacher says he is interested in anything you have to say and you believe him, but when you bring in your pet frog or your coin collection, he can't look at it because he has to go to a faculty meeting and discuss the needs of children.

We shall come back in a later chapter to the question of success, failure, anxiety, and frustration. For now, we would just like to note that in our view there is little sustained success in the cognitive domain by teachers who have not carefully attended to the affective domain. Conversely, there is little sustained success in the affective domain by teachers who have not carefully attended to the cognitive domain.

The testing of ends through the use of weekly, monthly, or annual exams is the device of the incompetent teacher. Good teachers need no such tests because at any given moment in any given lesson they know what each child is accomplishing. They get feedback. They read faces, they observe thought processes, they constantly assess what each child is doing, and they react to the child's work in such a way as to enable the child to solve his problems.

The good teachers understand that once they present a problem to a child, a number of responses are possible and they must react accordingly. A child can take many routes to an end. The teacher must know these routes and be prepared to assist the child. The good teacher sees himself in the employ of the minds of children, not the other way around. As a consequence children work for a good teacher—but that is not important. What is important is that they are working for themselves.

We are not suggesting here that the children determine educational ends. Educational ends are determined in many complex ways by the society, the community, the parents, the teachers, and the children. In most classrooms, however, the teacher determines many of the immediate or short-term objectives of instruction. To the extent that the teacher determines the ends, he must set up the conditions that enable the child to move to the accomplishment of the ends. But because there are many routes to the end, the teacher must constantly reorder the conditions so that they facilitate the route taken by the individual child.

The final point we should like to make relating to ends is that one should not set out ends that are not attainable by the children. We earnestly believe that children can attain much more than they are currently attaining in our schools. There are many reasons for this. We shan't go into these reasons here, with the exception of the unnecessary anxieties, frustrations, and conflicts already alluded to—and one other reason. Much of what we ask children to do can't be handled by elementary school children. They are often asked to handle hypothetical-deductive systems which they are constitutionally unable to handle, or they are asked to handle material in a form that they cannot handle. It is unfortunate that with all the child development courses that teachers are asked to take in college, few have studied the cognitive abilities of young children.

We have tried to make four points relating to ends, four points that need to be carefully examined by teachers. First, ends must be carefully thought out, as they are the reason for teaching. Second, knowledge ends and affective ends are reverse sides of the same coin. Third, within any lesson are a series of different paths or routes, all of which may lead to the teacher's ends. Fourth, before deciding to pursue an end the teacher must determine whether it is attainable in the first place and, if it is, under what conditions it can be attained.

chapter 5

Propositions and Pedagogy

All pedagogical techniques and teaching strategies, as well as all techniques and practices relating to changing or controlling student behavior, rest on fundamental propositions. Talk about planning for individual differences suggests that there are individual differences and these differences are significant. Detention halls suggest that those who believe in them hold a view of human nature from which the conclusion can be drawn that children learn from detention halls. Some teachers believe morality can be taught by telling children what correct behavior is. Some people believe that morality is taught by example and example only. Some believe both methods must be used. Each of these groups obviously hold a different set of propositions as to how children learn to behave morally. Many more illustrations can be supplied by the reader. We are only trying to illustrate the point that teachers do things for a reason, and that the reason is usually a fundamental belief about human nature and how humans learn and grow.

The problem, however, is that many teachers and curriculum writers do not think these basic propositions through, nor do they make them explicit—even to themselves. The failure to do so leads to all sorts of unsatisfactory consequences for children in our schools. One consequence is practices that contradict each other. The same school or teacher that believes each child is so unique that all instruction must be individualized will have a set of policies that punishes all children equally for the same infraction. Or a faculty that says a school is a place to make intellectual mistakes and that intellectual mistakes shouldn't be punished, but rather looked upon as an opportunity to learn, will turn around and punish third-graders who make social mistakes and will send home reports that punish both social and intellectual mistakes. Or a faculty will move to an ungraded program to let each child "grow at his own pace," and will then continue to speak of first-graders, second-graders, third-graders, etc. and will continue to group children, make blanket assignments, and carry out a number of other procedures that assume that "children grow at the same rate."

Another consequence of failing to identify basic propositions is that the teacher is left with only a vague "I believe" or "I think" or "I feel." He becomes dependent on workbooks or textbooks to carry him. He can never explain why any strategy works or fails. He is always looking for a new gimmick or for new materials. He can never develop his own strategies or his own materials. He fails with many children and defends himself by blaming the child, the home the child comes from, the child's past teachers, the number of students he has, the materials, or the other children. If the point is made that other children with the same characteristics from similar backgrounds, with similar teachers, in larger classrooms, and with poorer materials have succeeded and gone on to be huge successes in life, this teacher again has a handy set of pet clichés to save the day.

One of the most dangerous clichés is that after a child reaches a certain age he can't change. Education by definition has to do with change. No change, no education. It's that simple. It's surprising how many people believe that teaching and learning are unrelated phenomena. The failure to examine one's basic propositions can only lead to confusion, to a pedagogy that is rootless, to theory that is without cohesiveness, and to a failure to think systematically about how one teaches.

With the above in mind, we set out to list the fundamental propositions we hold, which we believe relate to teaching in that one will derive from them suggestions for how to behave as a teacher. As in the case of setting out ends, setting out basic principles has its pitfalls, not the least of which is that no matter how hard one tries, some fundamental beliefs probably remain hidden. But the advantages outweigh the problems. Among these advantages are:

1. Two teachers who disagree about how to teach and who also have correctly identified what they believe to be the nature of children and learning can at least understand the *basis* of their differences, by contrasting their beliefs.
2. If the fundamental propositions are based on solid social scientific evidence, then there is reason to believe that pedagogical practices derived from them will be sounder than those picked out of thin air.
3. Those practices that appear dubious in that one is not sure they ac-

complish anything, and also appear to be contradictory to a fundamental proposition based on solid evidence from another field, are more likely to be eliminated by teachers. Teachers are always looking for sound new methods. We need also to attend to the business of eliminating unsound methods.

4. By identifying basic propositions we can make the pedagogy proposed more understandable to others.

5. It is an open procedure and has the virtue of honesty.

6. In the process of stating one's fundamental propositions the list begins to grow and one is forced to view the teaching process as a more and more complex phenomenon. Things have a way of getting very complex and one is stunned by what one can't know. The value here is that simple answers following from one or two propositions are not possible. The teaching act *is* complex and he who would teach well must think hard.

PROPOSITIONS DEALING WITH CHILDREN'S RELATIONSHIPS TO REALITY

I. Elementary school children have certain logical structures with which they examine reality. These structures are:

Order. Asymmetrical relations (*A* is longer than *B*; *X* is the mother of *Y*) derive from the act of preparing and ordering objects according to some aspect in which they are perceived to differ.

Class. Classifying derives from the action of grouping objects together according to some aspect in which they are perceived to be similar.

Number. Numbers arise from the combining of classifying and ordering. Things which are similar are grouped together. Groups can be ordered according to their size.

Combinativity. Any two classes may be combined into one comprehensive class which embraces them both—e.g., $3 + 5 = 8$; all boys and all girls = all children. Moreover any two relationships $A > B$ and $B > C$ may be logically combined to form a new relationship, $A > C$.

Associativity. When several operations are to be combined, it makes no difference which are performed first—e.g., $(2 + 3) + (4 + 5) = 2 + (3 + 4) + 5$; (all girls and all boys) and all adults = all girls and (all boys and all adults).

Reversibility. Every logical or mathematical operation is reversible in the sense that there is an opposite operation that cancels it—e.g., $3 + 5 = 8$, but also $8 - 5 = 3$; all boys and all girls = all children, but all children except girls = all boys. These are examples of subtraction as the converse of addition. Similarly, division is the converse operation for multiplication—e.g., $3 \times 5 = 15$; but $15 \div 5 = 3$).[1]

Identity. When an operation is nullified by combining it with its opposite, leaving one at the point where one started, one has returned to the identity point—e.g., $0 + 3 - 3 = 0$, or $1 \times 5 \div 5 = 1$; I move 10 steps to the north then I move 10 steps to the south = I stand where I started. In the thought of the adult, making an hypothesis and subsequently rejecting it alters nothing, but the child cannot do this; the original data of a problem tend to be somewhat distorted by his having formulated an hypothesis even though he may discard it.

Tautology and iteration. Tautology holds for logical classes. Repeating a proposition, a classification, or a relation leaves it unchanged. Repeating a message may permit a listener to absorb the information, but the repeated message contains no more information than is contained in its first statement—e.g., all mammals and all mammals = all mammals; $A > B$, $A > B$, $= A > B$. Iteration holds for numbers. When a number is combined with itself, the result is a new number—e.g., $3 + 3 = 6$, and $3 \times 3 = 9$.

As the above structures arise in the development of the child he uses them to organize the reality he observes and the concepts he develops about that reality. The six-year-old can arrange sticks by length because he has the logical structure of order. The two-year-old cannot because he has yet to develop the structure of order. The elementary school child can see that subtraction undoes addition because of the logical structure of combinitivity and reversibility. The eight logical structures, then, are the means by which the child organizes and perceives the world.

II. The seven- to eleven-year-old produces knowledge through a process of interacting with reality. He does this in the following manner:

---

1 Piaget emphasizes reversibility as the most defined characteristic of mature thought or intelligence. Although motor habits and perceptions are capable of combination, they remain irreversible. Motor actions become reversible when the child ("sensorimotor stage 6") can retrace his steps, but such reversibility of action goes beyond habit and requires intelligence, as Piaget defines habits and intelligence. Images, like the habits and perceptions from which they derive, lack reversibility. It is only gradually, as central processes become more and more autonomous, that thought acquires this property of reversibility. The younger the child, the less reversible are his thought processes, and the more they resemble the sensorimotor patterns out of which they develop.

He observes concrete reality using his senses.

He makes factual statements about the observed reality.

He inductively relates these factual statements to each other to produce generalizations, using his logical structures.

He can deduce other generalizations, by relating two or more statements arrived at inductively.

In the process of observing reality the observer brings to bear on the reality whatever concepts he may have that may be relevant to describing the reality being observed.

III. Two conditions may exist vis-à-vis the concepts in the child's mind and the reality that is in the world when the child interacts with reality:

The first is that the two may be in agreement.

The second is that there will be a contradiction between the concepts in the child's mind and the reality he is observing.

IV. When the first condition (in III, above) exists over an extended period of time, boredom results.

V. When the second condition (in III, above) exists, the child deals with the contradiction in one of three ways:

The child may block the contradiction out; the contradiction between the child's concepts and reality may be too great for the child to deal with and he will give up.

The child may assimilate. That is to say, he may change the reality to fit his concepts.

The child may accommodate. In accommodating the child alters his concepts to match reality.

Assimilation and accommodation go on simultaneously. We use the term *assimilate* when the predominant activity is assimilation. Divergent thinking would be a possible result in this case. When the child is doing a minimum of assimilation and a maximum of accommodation we use the term *accommodation* to describe his actions. Convergent thinking might be a result in this case. When there is an equal amount of assimilating and accommodating going on we have equilibrium, or intelligent adaptation.

When the predominant activity is assimilation the child exhibits a great deal of imagination. When his activity is predominantly accommodating he is doing a great deal of imitating. When he is close to equilibrium his activity is best described as scientific problem solving.

PROPOSITIONS DEALING WITH THE ROLE
OF THE TEACHER

Learning, then, is a result of the child interacting with physical reality and of making an adjustment to reality that leads to new or modified concepts. Children learn all of the time. Formal education or schooling differs from other education. In formal education what is to be learned has been predetermined by someone else (usually a teacher) and that someone else has selected and organized the reality with which he believes it is necessary for the child to interact for the particular learning to take place. To put it another way, the teacher's task has four aspects. Each of these aspects can be stated in at least two ways, depending on how much self-direction by students is desired.

If the teacher is the sole director of learning, then the teacher's task can be stated as follows:

VI. The teacher must determine what concept he wishes the child to learn.

VII. The teacher must determine what reality will yield that concept if the child interacts with the reality.

VIII. The teacher must endeavor to get the child to interact with the reality.

IX. The teacher must endeavor to keep the child interacting until all contradictions between the child's concepts and reality are resolved.

Let us comment briefly upon each of these and return to them for a more extended treatment in the chapters that follow. Society imposes some limitations on the concepts to be learned by an elementary school child. The child's cognitive ability also imposes some limitations. Elementary school children can learn anything that can be arrived at inductively through an examination of concrete reality. A concrete reality will yield demonstrative facts. A concrete reality can be organized through imposing the logical structures of the child.

Concepts that are derived logically from abstract assumptions or postulates will not be understood by children of this age. The child must be able to connect his concept to reality. Given two related propositions that the child knows to be true (i.e., that are a result of his observations), the child can draw the implication and arrive at the conclusion. He will not, however, draw a correct implication if he believes one or more of the related propositions are false. The teacher must, then, screen the concepts he wishes to teach by acting in accordance with proposition VII. That is, once a determination has been made to teach concept X the teacher needs to try to arrange some reality in which the concept is embedded. The most effective way of accomplishing this is for the teacher to pose to himself the question: What concrete evidence is needed from which I can derive the concept or concepts I wish to teach? Suppose the teacher wishes the children to acquire the following concept: *In English there is a correspondence in number between nouns and their determiners.* The question the teacher must ask is: What reality do I select that will result in the child seeing this concept? Obviously, the reality must deal with nouns and determiners. Furthermore, the children must: recognize a noun; recognize the noun's determiner; have a concept of number; recognize that determiners and nouns say something about number.

In the sample sentence, "All boys eat candy," the child can then label "All" as the determiner for "boy" and state that there is more than one boy. In fact, the statement is talking about all boys. Given this one sentence, however, one cannot conclude that there is a correspondence in number between nouns and their determiners. The teacher must now offer more data. The additional data might be:

A girl ran home.
An apple a day keeps the doctor away.
Two men are working in a factory.
Many children play baseball.
Etc.

The teacher may present the above data to the child and ask: What similarity is there between nouns and determiners? The child may or may not see the concept of correspondence of number at this point—but that doesn't concern us here. What is relevant here is that the correspondence of number between noun and determiner can be concluded from the evidence, if not as a final conclusion, then at least as a working hypothesis.

Summarizing to this point, then, the teacher's task is first to decide on the concept he wishes to teach and second to determine what data or reality is necessary to infer the concept, given the relevant concepts the child already has and the means or structure he has for organizing the data so that the concept is revealed to him.

Alternatively, if the child is directly involved in deciding what he will learn, as may occur in many "open" classrooms, then the teacher's task may be stated as follows:

VI-a. The teacher must explore with the child the problems with which the child wishes to deal. The teacher needs to know what concepts or ideas are related to or contained in the problems raised by the child.

VII-a. The teacher must explore with the child the possible ways of approaching the problem.

VIII-a. The teacher must allow the child to wrestle with the problem selected.

IX-a. The teacher must support the child when the going gets tough.

Let us comment briefly on this alternative set of statements about the teacher's task. If the teacher believes that the child should be involved in deciding what is to be learned, then the teacher must be willing to enlarge his own background and knowledge considerably. He needs to know the variety of learnings that are inherent in a wide range of problems which the child may select to pursue. He needs to know the possible sources of information that exist, so that he can help the child to increase his options as regards ways of approaching the problem.

The teacher must be willing to let the child make "poor" decisions, to let him start down a "dead end" course of investigation rather than redirect him at the beginning. And when the child reaches the barrier at that dead end, the teacher needs to provide acceptance of failure and encouragement to try another path.

Beyond this the teacher should realize that children differ in the amount of self-direction they need or want. For some children the most comfortable and productive kind of decision will be to choose among options that the teacher has provided. For others the productive decision will be to choose among alternatives generated by themselves and their peers.

PROPOSITIONS DEALING WITH MOTIVATION

The whole process of learning hinges, of course, on the child's drive to learn. Volumes have been written on motivating the child to learn and teachers have long lamented the child who could if he only would. Our own view is that much of this discussion has been misleading and sometimes irrelevant. The key to the problem rests with two propositions:

X. In the American culture one quickly learns that he is applauded when he succeeds and booed—or at least ignored—when he fails.

XI. It is the basic nature of human beings to learn.

Success is in part intellectual, in part a matter of psychomotor skill, and in part a matter of affect. What happens to the young child following his natural bent for knowledge is that those around him who give the affect (approval and disapproval) for his successes and failures often require a higher rate of success than he intellectually is capable of achieving. But the very nature of knowledge seeking is such that one must fail more often than one succeeds. As the physicist Michael Faraday wrote:[2]

The world little knows how many of the thoughts and theories which have passed through the mind of a scientific investigator have been crushed in silence and secrecy by his own severe criticisms and adverse examinations; that in the most successful instances not a tenth of the suggestions, the hopes, the wishes, the preliminary conclusions have been realized.

Einstein on the same point said:

Looking back . . . over the long and labyrinthine path which finally led to the discovery [of the quantum theory], I am vividly reminded of Goethe's saying that men will always be making mistakes as long as they are striving after something.

Einstein again:

These were errors in thinking which caused me two years of hard work before at last, in 1915, I recognized them as such. . . . The final results appear almost simple; any intelligent undergraduate can understand them without much trouble. But the years of searching in the dark for a truth that one feels, but cannot express; the intense desire and the alternations of confidence and misgiving, until one breaks through to clarity and understanding, are only known to him who has himself experienced them.

And Darwin observed:

I have steadily endeavored to keep my mind free so as to give up any hypothesis, however much beloved (and I cannot resist forming one on every subject), as soon as facts are shown to be opposed to it. . . . I cannot remember a single first-formed hypothesis which had not after a time to be given up or be greatly modified.

Hermann von Helmholtz, in discussing his intellectual successes, wrote:

I am fain to compare myself with a wanderer on the mountains who, not knowing the path, climbs slowly and painfully upwards and often has to retrace his steps because he can go no further—then, whether by taking thought or from luck, discovers a new track that leads him on a little till at length when he reaches the summit he finds to his shame that there is a royal road, by which he might have ascended, had he only had the wits to find the right approach to it.[3]

[2] The following quotations of Faraday, Einstein, and Darwin are in W. I. B. Beveridge, *The Art of Scientific Investigation* (New York: Random House, 1957), pp. 79, 81, 79, 80 respectively.

[3] Reprinted from *Hermann von Helmholtz*, by L. Koenigsberger (1906), trans. by F. A. Welby (Oxford: Clarendon Press).

We have taken the space to quote these scholars because above all else they were thinkers of the first order, and yet they failed repeatedly. The advantage they and others like them have over young children is that they learned that failure was unavoidable. Indeed, it seems clear that they didn't view their failure as failure but rather as necessary steps on the way to truth. Edison is alleged to have said to an assistant who complained that no progress was being made toward finding a suitable light filament that in fact much progress had been made because they now knew of a great many materials that were unsuitable as filaments. Everywhere, then, the scholar profits by his mistakes.

The world of the school, however, often fails to understand this. Children are expected to move inexorably to the "correct" concept and woe to those who don't follow the straight line to truth. They fail. They fail not only because they do not stick to the royal road but also on occasion because they travel the royal road too slowly.

What the teacher must do relating to these matters is to first redefine success in terms that scholars would understand. He must give support to the child who will risk a hypothesis, and give support to the child who will disprove and give up his pet hypothesis. He must recognize that these two steps are necessary to producing knowledge, and consequently belong in a room devoted to learning.

Learning will not come to the child who is so afraid of failure that he will not attack any problems. Our experience is that children are caught between the desire to learn on one hand and the fear of failure on the other. The same child who learns little in school, where all failures are made public, noted in permanent records, and communicated to parents and others, memorizes the batting averages of two hundred major league ballplayers and solves all sorts of other problems outside school, where learning is a private matter and no records are kept, and where one can keep failing until one succeeds. We might note also that in most of the out-of-school problems reality can be dealt with because it is concrete.

One of the teacher's tasks is to endeavor to get the child to interact with reality. In carrying out this task the teacher must be cognizant of the propositions relating to motivation and success.

PROPOSITIONS RELATING TO VALUES

To keep the child interacting with reality the teacher must attend to values the child holds. Einstein's statement, quoted earlier, that "the years of searching in the dark for a truth that one feels, but cannot express; the intense desire and the alternations of confidence and misgiving, until one breaks through to clarity and understanding, are only known to him who has himself experienced them," reveals what is required here.

And Helmholtz could have pointed out that some "wanderers on the mountain" give up when things get a little too difficult.

The question is: What sustains men in their quest for knowledge? The answer is that they value the search, they value the solution, they value the rewards that come with a final solution, the rewards that come from their peers as well as the inner rewards that come with the changing of doubt to a satisfactory solution:

XII. To pursue knowledge one must value knowledge and value the pursuit.

Children who actively pursue knowledge over long periods of time have learned a set of attitudes and values that view the pursuit as worthy of the price that must be paid. The price is temporary failure, anxiety, time, effort and the rest that goes into scholarship. Those who will not pursue it but prefer sports to scholarship, fooling around to paying attention, playing hooky to attending school, obviously do not value learning. They may pay lip service to learning but they won't pay the price. Often, they will work very hard at other matters but not at schooling or "book learning." The reason is that they have learned to value these other activities much more than they value learning.

XIII. Learning activities that lead to knowledge are only possible where values and attitudes necessary to learning are present.

Two points are necessary here. First, many children pursue knowledge not as an end but as a means. They may study because Mother is good, Mother says to study, and they wish to please Mother. They may study because they want to be a success in life and they believe that success is a function of study. These students tend to be other-directed students and when the external pressures are off they tend to give up the pursuit of knowledge. They rarely become independent scholars in the sense that they can define a problem by themselves and move to solution. In our other-directed schools most good students are of this type.

It follows then that if we are to develop scholars and thinkers who can function independently, we must reach the point with children where they internalize the values and attitudes necessary to sustain intellectual activity.

The second point we wish to make is that as the complexity of the intellectual task and the length of time needed to solve the task increase, the amount of commitment needed to sustain the activity and the amount of frustration the individual must handle are both increased. Teachers need, for example, little commitment to sustain activity through a workshop on the teaching of mathematics. It takes a great deal of commitment and sacrifice to pursue a master's degree. It takes still more to pursue a doctorate. Many who have the intelligence and the skills to handle the intellectual tasks of meeting the requirements of doctoral programs lack the commitment to scholarship, lack the ability to handle the frustrations involved, and lack the desire to persevere over a long period of time. The external pressures that are there to get a bachelor's degree are not there to sustain the activity necessary for a doctorate. Alas, few of us have been taught by the schools to be independent and few of us have been taught the values necessary to carry out any extended intellectual activity.[4]

PROPOSITIONS RELATING TO CLASSROOM ENVIRONMENT

All of the above discussion leads us to three major propositions:

XIV. There is an ideal set of conditions under which children can produce knowledge.

XV. There is an ideal set of conditions under which children can develop the values and attitudes necessary for sustained knowledge-producing activity.

XVI. Conditions necessary for attaining both sets of ends must operate simultaneously in the classroom if children are to learn to be independent knowledge producers.

Children, we have said, learn knowledge by moving from the concrete to the abstract. Values, we suspect, are learned in much the same manner. Part of the concrete reality of the classroom is the teacher. What children observe the teacher valuing, they will tend to value. Note we say what the children *observe*. It is not just a matter of teachers *saying* that they value reading, mathematics, history, thinking, etc. Teachers need to demonstrate through their actions that they value scholarship, the novel, the indeterminate situation, the excitement of moving from the known to the unknown, the untested hypothesis, or a unique solution. The trouble with most classrooms is that there is no evidence that anyone in the room, including the teacher, values the production of knowledge for themselves. The evidence often suggests that the teacher values having the children gain knowledge, but little to

---

[4] Benjamin Bloom et al., *Taxonomy of Educational Objectives, The Classification of Educational Goals, Handbook I: Cognitive Domain* (New York: David McKay Company, 1956) and David R. Krathwohl et al., *Taxonomy of Educational Objectives, The Classification of Educational Goals, Handbook II: Affective Domain* (New York: David McKay Company, 1964) make excellent reading for those who would understand the ever-increasing complexity of intellectual behavior and value-oriented behavior.

suggest that the teacher values gaining knowledge himself. It is all too often a case of "Do as I say, not as I do."

Teachers would do well to hang their degrees on the wall of the room, as well as examples of the children's work. They would do well to have part of their personal library in the room, and they would do even better to be caught reading a book once in a while by their pupils. They would do well to say, "I don't know," when they don't know. They would do well to say, "Let me see if I can figure that out," and then spend some time thinking out loud while they try to solve a problem. It would even be beneficial if sometimes they were unable to come to an immediate conclusion but had to pursue an answer for several days, or a week, or even a semester before disposing of the problem.

It would be good for children to see a teacher's hypothesis fail to bear fruit, just as their hypotheses often fail to bear fruit. It wouldn't hurt one bit for children to see a teacher come up against an intellectual stone wall, but refuse to quit in the face of frustration. One way for children to learn how to solve problems is for them to see someone else solving problems. One way for children to learn to value the thinking life is for them to see someone who values the thinking life. A teacher who is excited about learning, and who shows he values learning, is worth ten teachers who value children but care little for learning. To value children is a fine trait and it may even be a necessary condition for being a good teacher, but it isn't a sufficient condition. To be a teacher one must also value learning and the pursuit of knowledge.

chapter 6

Modes of Discovery*

In the last several chapters we have been using the term *discovery* very loosely. We are not alone in this. The fact that many educators are talking about "discovery" does not mean that they are speaking the same language. Lack of a common meaning for the term *discovery* has contributed to controversy over the use of discovery as an instructional method. For example, there is disagreement over the use of verbal discussion in connection with discovery lessons. Hendrix believes that "nonverbal awareness" is an important aspect of the discovery process, and argues that children should not verbalize their discoveries too rapidly.[1] Suchman, on the other hand, believes that giving children practice in verbalizing, or asking the right questions, will improve their ability to discover.[2]

There is also disagreement as to the appropriate age level for use of discovery methods. Bruner argues that very young children can discover certain basic concepts, and that this process can be used to advantage with children in both elementary and secondary schools.[3] Ausubel admits the possibility that learning by discovery may be effective in the elementary school, but feels that the student in secondary school would absorb more if taught by other methods.[4]

---

* This chapter was originally published in *Theory into Practice,* February 1969 issue.

[1] Gertrude Hendrix, "Prerequisite to Meaning," *The Mathematics Teacher* 43 (1950): 339.

[2] J. Richard Suchman, "Inquiry Training: Building Skills for Autonomous Discovery," *Merrill-Palmer Quarterly of Behavior and Development* 7 (1961): 169.

[3] Jerome S. Bruner, *The Process of Education* (Cambridge: Harvard University Press, 1960).

[4] David P. Ausubel, "Learning by Discovery: Rationale and Mystique," *National Association of Secondary School Principal's Bulletin* 45 (December 1961): 20.

Surely there is a crucial difference between teaching techniques which encourage nonverbal processes of discovery and teaching techniques which encourage highly verbal processes of discovery. Furthermore, there must be a distinct difference between strategies which encourage a six-year-old's discovery and strategies which encourage a sixteen-year-old's discovery. Yet educators go on talking about "the discovery method" as if it were a single method, as if there were only one kind of discovery process being used by teachers.

The thesis to be advanced here is that different kinds of discovery lessons are appropriate for achieving different types of objectives, for dealing with different types of subject matter, and for use with children at different levels of cognitive ability. It might be fruitful for teachers to view the different types of discovery lessons with these aspects in mind. If one begins by considering the epistemological notion of different kinds of inquiry, it is possible to distinguish at least three "modes" of discovery, which can be used to differentiate six kinds of discovery lessons currently being taught in our schools at one level or another.

INDUCTIVE DISCOVERY

Inductive discovery is the mode of discovery to which most contemporary educators refer when they discuss the discovery method. Inductive discovery involves the collection and reordering of data to arrive at a new category, concept, or generalization. It is the method of discovery used in the descriptive stage of science. Two types of lessons which use the inductive mode of discovery can be identified.

The *open inductive discovery lesson* is one whose chief aim is to give children experience in a particular process of inquiry: the process of categorization. There is no particular category or generalization which the teacher expects the children to discover. The lesson is directed at "learning how to learn," in the sense of learning to organize data.

Perhaps it should be noted here that categorizing ability is developed gradually in children between the ages of four and eight. Young children will frequently group objects on the basis of color or form, or both. However, they are generally unable to form logical categories, which take account of hierarchial relationships.[5] For example, a five-year-old will make piles of blue circles, red circles, blue squares, and red squares, and consider each pile as a separate group. An eight-year-old will note that the blue circles and red circles are subgroups of the larger class of

---

[5] Barbel Inhelder and Jean Piaget, *The Early Growth of Logic in the Child* (New York: Harper and Row, 1964), p. 117.

circles. According to Inhelder and Piaget, true classification occurs only when the child is aware of this hierarchy of classes and subclasses.[6]

An example of the open inductive discovery lesson would be one in which children are given pictures of various kinds of foods and are asked to group them. Some children might categorize them as "breakfast foods," "lunch foods," and "supper foods." Others might group the foods as meats, vegetables, fruits, dairy products, etc. Still others might group on the basis of color, or texture, or place of origin. All of the groupings could be considered to be correct. Discussion of the results could lead to an awareness that different category systems serve different purposes, or that some categories are discrete and others are not.

This kind of lesson could be used with many types of materials and would not need to be tied in with any particular subject matter. It could be used in connection with almost any study which involves categorization.

This type of lesson is appropriate from the kindergarten or first grade on. Many of the younger children will not be able to form logical categories (according to Inhelder and Piaget), but the process of trying to group will provide them with experiences which can contribute to the later development of their ability to categorize.

This type of lesson can be developed from some very simple materials and activities that are not necessarily "new" to the curriculum. The collection of interesting items on a nature walk and the subsequent grouping of these items by individual children is an example of one such activity. One teacher reports that one child, having collected leaves, seeds, sticks, and grasses, placed them in three categories: "green things," which included the leaves and seeds; "long things," which included the sticks; and "long, green things," which included the grasses.

The open inductive discovery lesson, then, is one in which the child is relatively free to shape the data in his own ways. It is hoped that by doing this he is learning to observe the world around him and to organize it for his own purposes.

The *structured inductive discovery lesson* is one whose chief aim is to have children attain a particular concept. The primary focus is acquisition of subject matter, within the framework of the discovery approach.

An example of this type of lesson would be one in which children are presented with a series of pictures of people in different kinds of group situations, such as:

> Group I: A family around a dinner table
> Two girls playing with dolls
> A mother bathing a baby

[6] *Ibid.,* p. 47.

Group II: Boy Scouts at a meeting
             A Little League baseball team playing a game
             Girls at a dancing class
Group III: Fans at a football game
             Commuters waiting at the train station
             Swimmers at the beach

Children might then be shown three more pictures and asked to place each in the group with which it belonged. These pictures might include shoppers in a store, a father reading a story to two children, and a group of children working in a classroom.

The discussion of the pictures would deal with similarities among groups and differences between groups. Eventually the concepts of primary, secondary, and nonintegrated groups would be developed.

The structured inductive discovery lesson utilizes concrete or representational materials. Concepts from the descriptive sciences are developed. Anthropology, sociology, geography, biology, and structural linguistics are some of the subject areas which can be taught through this type of lesson.

One characteristic which distinguishes the structured inductive lesson from all other types of discovery lesson is the importance of the organization of data. The concepts which have been developed in the descriptive sciences are not simply the result of the data that were observed. Rather, the concepts have been shaped by the perceptions of the observers. The probability that Linnaeus's system of classification would be duplicated by another biologist observing the same data is relatively small. There are too many bases for classification available in such a set of data.

The same situation exists for the student who is presented with data in any discovery lesson. Therefore, if the teacher hopes to have particular concepts developed effectively and efficiently, it is important that the data be organized in a way that structures the perceptions of the observers. Since the amount of data also affects the outcome of inductive discovery,[7] it is necessary to provide children with sufficient amounts of data. This will tend to increase the chances of most children arriving at the same conclusion.

The structured inductive discovery lesson is appropriate for use with children as soon as they are able to classify concrete materials in a logical fashion. According to Piaget, this ability develops at around seven or eight years of age.[8] At an earlier level of cognitive development children

---

[7] Greta G. Morine, "A Model of Inductive Discovery for Instructional Theory" (Ed.D. diss., Teachers College, Columbia University, 1965), p. 142.

[8] John J. Flavell, *The Developmental Psychology of Jean Piaget* (Princeton, N.J.: D. Van Nostrand Company, 1963), chapter 8.

could do some grouping of materials, but probably would not be able to form logical categories. Students in secondary schools can still profit from this type of lesson when they are being introduced to new subject matter, since they will tend to operate at a simpler cognitive level in their understanding of new materials than in their understanding of familiar material.

Many of the newer curriculum materials in the social sciences are designed around the structured inductive discovery lesson. The Geography Learning Labs produced by the Learning Center in Princeton, New Jersey (Creative Playthings, Inc.) are examples of these kinds of materials. They provide the teacher with concrete materials and/or organized data that can be utilized to help children develop particular key concepts relevant to the study of geography.

The structured inductive discovery lesson and the open inductive discovery lesson have certain important similarities. Chief among these is the fact that the child thinks inductively in both. The major difference between the open and the structured inductive discovery lesson is the objective being stressed. The chief aim of the open inductive lesson is to train children in the use of the inductive process of inquiry, while the structured inductive lesson primarily aims at developing understanding of basic concepts. (It might be noted here that *all* discovery lessons share a secondary aim of encouraging children to think for themselves.)

This difference in the primary aims of the open and structured inductive discovery lessons leads to a difference in the organization of materials by the teacher. In the open inductive discovery lesson, materials can be presented to the child in a random order. The child organizes the materials, and divergent results are of value in discussion of categorization as a process of inquiry. In the structured inductive discovery lesson, materials must be organized before they are presented to the child in order to facilitate discovery of the particular concept being developed.

DEDUCTIVE DISCOVERY

The traditional explanation of the difference between induction and deduction is that the former moves from the specific to the general, while the latter moves from the general to the specific. In deductive discovery one might assume that this distinction would continue to hold. Deductive discovery would involve the combining or relating of general ideas in order to arrive at specific statements, as in the construction of a syllogism.

In discussing discovery methods related to the teaching of mathematics Henderson presents a fictitious example of deductive discovery.[9] This technique of instruction involves asking questions which lead the student to form logical syllogisms, which can result in the student's correction of inaccurate statements he has made. This is the meaning of deductive discovery which Henderson says is shared by Hendrix and Beberman, and which is utilized in the research of the University of Illinois Committee on School Mathematics (UICSM) that Beberman directed.

This procedure might be called the *simple deductive discovery method.* A more familiar name for it would be the Socratic method. In this type of lesson the teacher tends to control the data being used by students, since his questions must be designed to elicit propositions which lead logically to a particular conclusion.

In this approach the student must think deductively, and the materials are essentially abstract. That is, the student is dealing with relationships among verbal propositions. For this reason the simple deductive discovery method is appropriate for children in Piaget's stage of "formal operations," which usually begins at eleven or twelve years of age. At this time, Piaget suggests, children are able to reason deductively and to operate upon verbal propositions.[10] One would not expect this method to be effective in the earlier stages of cognitive development.

The primary aim of this type of lesson is to have students learn certain accepted conclusions or principles. However, these conclusions are developed by having the student utilize the deductive process of inquiry, rather than by simply stating the conclusion. Students are encouraged to look for logical contradictions between general statements, and thus, to question their conclusions. As Henderson points out, some of the UICSM materials are designed to be used in conjunction with the simple deductive discovery method.[11] The method can also be used with subjects such as physics and chemistry, which are deductive sciences.

Henderson seems to imply that there is only one deductive discovery method, the one which we have here labeled the simple deductive discovery method. However, it is possible to identify two more deductive discovery methods.

The *semideductive discovery lesson* is similar to the structured inductive discovery lesson in many ways. The aim is to have children develop and learn basic concepts in a particular field of study. These concepts are arrived at inductively, by the children, through use of concrete or representational materials. The major difference is in the nature of

---

9 Kenneth B. Henderson, "Research on Teaching Secondary School Mathematics," in *Handbook of Research on Teaching,* ed. N. L. Gage (Chicago: Rand McNally and Company, 1963), pp. 1007–30.

10 Flavell, *Jean Piaget,* chapter 6.

11 Henderson, "Secondary School Mathematics," p. 1010.

the subject matter itself. The concepts to be discovered were originally developed in a deductive system of knowledge.

An example of a semideductive discovery lesson would be one in which children are asked to list twenty whole numbers of their own choosing. They might then be directed to divide each number by 2. Finally, they might be told to see how many different remainders they have, and to group the numbers according to remainder. When the class compared results they would find that they had two groups of numbers: those with remainders of 0, called even numbers; those with remainders of 1, called odd numbers.

The children would have arrived at these two categories by observing specific examples. But the data they would have observed would be in large part selected by the children themselves, rather than by the teacher. The selection of the original twenty numbers is not crucial to the development of the categories. Any set of numbers will yield the same results, since the numbers are elements of a deductive system. The outcome (the children's generalization) is determined by the rules of the system, rather than by the selection and organization of the data.

The semideductive discovery lesson is unique in that children are thinking inductively in a deductive system. They arrive at rules or properties by observing specific data rather than by constructing deductive chains of statements, as the theoretician might. But the rules or properties which they can discover are controlled by the system in which they are working. The system (that is, the elements to be worked with and the operation to be utilized) limits the possible outcomes. The educational result is that the process of teaching is simplified, because the probability that children will arrive at an unexpected conclusion is greatly reduced.

As was mentioned earlier, in a structured inductive discovery lesson the teacher or the curriculum planner must select and organize data with great care, since concepts developed in a descriptive (inductive) system of knowledge do not follow directly from the data. Different concepts or categories might be developed which would be just as logically valid. In the semideductive discovery lesson, however, the selection of data is a simple task once one can determine the concept to be taught. The concept does follow directly from the data (the "givens") in a prescriptive (deductive) system.

The semideductive discovery lesson deals, therefore, with concepts developed in areas of knowledge such as mathematics and physics, which are deductive systems. Since the process of thought utilized by children is inductive, however, this type of lesson can most appropriately be taught during what Piaget calls the "concrete" stage of cognitive development, that is, from the age of seven or eight to the age of eleven or twelve.

It is probably no accident that the semideductive discovery lesson is the type around which the greatest number of curriculum materials have been designed. It is easier to develop teaching materials for this type of lesson than for the structured inductive discovery lesson, since selection and organization of data is not so crucial. The modern mathematics materials, which utilize the discovery approach, such as the Cuisenaire rods, are examples of these kinds of materials. So also are many of the science programs, such as those developed by Educational Services Incorporated, which encourage children's experimentation with given materials, such as weights and balances.

The *hypotheticodeductive discovery lesson* is one in which children themselves utilize a deductive mode of thought. In general, this will involve hypothesizing as to causes and relationships or predicting results. Testing of the hypothesis or prediction would also be an essential part of the lesson.

An example of this type of lesson would be one in which students are shown a traditional experiment, such as a can of water being heated, sealed, and cooled, with the resultant collapse of the can. They might then be asked to determine what aspects of the procedure could not be changed without changing the results. This would require that they identify the variables and change them one at a time, or in other words, test the effect of each variable.

Because hypotheses would need to be tested against reality, concrete materials would frequently be required in the hypotheticodeductive discovery lesson. Also, since hypotheses are advanced by the child, he tends to exert some control over the specific data with which he will work. Subject matter to be dealt with could include the natural sciences, as well as those social sciences which have well-developed deductive theories.

This type of lesson is appropriate for children of eleven or twelve, or older, who have reached the "formal" stage of cognitive development. According to Piaget, children in earlier stages would not have the ability to control variables in order to test their hypotheses.[12] It is important to note also that the primary aim of this type of lesson would probably be for children to learn investigative techniques. As Ausubel suggests, it would be very time-consuming to teach all subject matter by this procedure when students have the cognitive ability to understand and operate with abstract materials. Some concepts will be developed as a result of the hypotheses being tested; other concepts may perhaps be more efficiently developed through written materials or oral discussions.

The Suchman materials for use in inquiry training, now published

[12] Flavell, *Jean Piaget,* chapter 5.

by Science Research Associates, are an example of curriculum materials which are available for this type of lesson.[13]

The three types of deductive discovery lessons are similar in that all deal with knowledge which has been developed through use of a deductive mode of inquiry. They differ in two important ways. The semideductive discovery lesson requires only inductive thinking by the child, and can be utilized during the developmental period of concrete operations (age seven to eleven). Its major aim is to have children learn basic concepts. The simple deductive discovery lesson and the hypotheticodeductive discovery lesson both require that the child think deductively, and thus cannot be effectively utilized prior to the stage of formal operations (age eleven or twelve and beyond). The major aim of both the simple deductive and hypotheticodeductive discovery lessons is to have children learn to utilize deductive methods of inquiry effectively.

TRANSDUCTIVE DISCOVERY

Piaget defines *transductive thinking* as the relating of sets of data in nonlogical ways.[14] Transductive reasoning moves from particular to particular. For example, a young child may learn that red means "you stop" and green means "you go," then reason transductively that orange means "you eat it." The particulars being associated here are a color and an activity performed in relation to an object of that color. Another product of transductive reasoning would be the line "The fog comes on little cat feet. . . ." Here particular characteristics of fog are related to particular characteristics of a cat.

In transductive thinking the child relates or compares two particular items and notes that they are similar in one or more ways. For example, a kangaroo is like an opossum because they both carry their babies in pouches. A giraffe is like an ostrich because they both have big necks. A car is like a racehorse because they both go fast.

Transductive thinking may lead to overgeneralization or stereotyped thinking, and thus many people suggest that it is nonlogical thinking. However, the same process can lead to divergent or imaginative perceptions of the world, and thus many people characterize transductive thinking as highly creative.

Piaget points out that this type of reasoning is typical of the child in the "preoperational" stage of cognitive development, that is, prior to

---

[13] Richard Suchman, *Inquiry Development Program in Physical Science, Grades 6–9* (Chicago: Science Research Associates, 1968).
[14] Flavell, *Jean Piaget*, chapter 4.

the age of seven or eight.[15] However, at this stage the reasoning is not controlled by the child, rather the child is "controlled" by the reasoning. The ability to reason transductively is retained at later stages of development, and in these later stages the child has somewhat more control over his use of transductive reasoning. As Flavell puts it:

> The preoperational child is the child of wonder; his cognition appears to us naive, impression-bound, and poorly organized. There is an essential lawlessness about his world without, of course, this fact in any way entering his awareness to inhibit the zest and flights of fancy with which he approaches new situations. . . . The child of concrete operations can be caricatured as a sober and bookkeeperish organizer of the real and a distruster of the subtle, the elusive, and the hypothetical. The adolescent has something of both. . . . Unlike the concrete-operational child, he can soar; but also unlike the preoperational child, it is a controlled and planned soaring.[16]

Transductive reasoning is more commonly referred to as imaginative or artistic thinking. It is the type of thinking that produces analogy or metaphor. As Flavell suggests above, it is a type of thinking which is most effectively controlled by the child in the formal operations stage.

The *transductive discovery lesson* is one in which children are encouraged to use transductive thinking. The general aim of the lesson would be to develop skill in artistic methods of inquiry.

This type of lesson is appropriate in dealing with literary composition as well as composition in the fields of music or arts and crafts. Materials would vary from the concrete, in dealing with arts and crafts or improvisation with musical instruments, to the abstract, in composing songs, stories, or poems. In either case the selection and organization of "data" or specific materials would be largely controlled by the child.

The transductive discovery lesson is perhaps most commonly exemplified in the "creative writing" lesson. It is a type of lesson which is not generally considered when educators discuss "the discovery lesson." And yet the factors which affect discovery in the transductive lesson are strikingly similar to those which affect discovery in the inductive and deductive discovery lessons. These would include such things as the type of materials, the child's familiarity with the materials, and the amount of time available for experimentation with the materials, to mention only a few.[17]

If we accept Flavell's statement above, then it would seem to follow that the most effective transductive discovery lessons could be taught to children in the formal operations stage. They would be most adept at

---

[15] Ibid.
[16] Ibid., p. 211.
[17] Morine, "A Model of Inductive Discovery," pp. 110–13.

controlling their use of this particular mode of reasoning. Transductive discovery lessons can also be taught to children in the concrete operational stage, particularly when concrete materials are used, but teachers should expect the productions of these children to be much more closely tied to reality.

This analysis of differences and similarities among the six types of discovery lessons within the three main modes of discovery seems to indicate clearly that it is not reasonable to talk about "the discovery lesson" as if it were a single entity. For effective utilization of methods of teaching which involve active inquiry by children—i.e., discovery methods—it would seem to be important for educators to differentiate among the kinds of lessons in terms of their appropriateness for dealing with different areas of knowledge, for use with children of different cognitive abilities, and for achieving different educational aims. Such a clarification in use of terms might also help educational researchers in their attempts to evaluate the results of learning by discovery methods.

Procedures as to organization and selection of data in the various types of discovery lessons differ somewhat. Most notably, in the structured inductive discovery lesson the data must be carefully selected and organized beforehand if there is to be efficient learning of subject matter. In the simple deductive discovery lesson the teacher also preselects and controls the data through certain questions. In the semideductive discovery lesson the system of knowledge controls the available data as well as the possible conclusions, so preselection of data by the teacher or curriculum planner is not so important, although the organization of data will still be controlled by the teacher. In the open inductive discovery lesson, the hypotheticodeductive discovery lesson, and the transductive discovery lesson, where the emphasis is on learning a method of inquiry, the student is generally free to select and organize data within a framework or limitations determined by the teacher.

SUMMARY

Three basic modes of discovery have been identified: the inductive, the deductive, and the transductive. Within this framework, six types of discovery lessons have been described. These differ in relation to: the type of inquiry used to develop knowledge in the discipline to be taught; the type of thinking to be utilized by the student; the stage of cognitive development required of the student; the primary aim or purpose of the lesson. The differences can be diagramed as shown in Table 6–1.

TABLE 6–1

Type of Discovery Lesson	Type of Inquiry in Discipline to be Taught	Type of Thinking Utilized by Student	Cognitive Development Required of Student	Primary Aim of Lesson
Open inductive	Descriptive or inductive (e.g., anthropology, sociology, geography)	Inductive thought	Intuitive or concrete stage (ages 6–11)	To teach inductive method of inquiry (categorizing)
Structured inductive	Descriptive or inductive	Inductive thought	Concrete or formal stage (ages 8 and beyond)	To teach subject matter (concepts, categories, generalizations)
Semideductive	Prescriptive or deductive (e.g., mathematics, physics)	Inductive thought	Concrete or formal stage (ages 8 and beyond)	To teach subject matter (properties, concepts)
Simple deductive	Prescriptive or deductive	Deductive thought	Formal stage (age 11 or 12 and beyond)	To teach subject matter (conclusions derived from basic premises)
Hypotheticodeductive	Prescriptive or deductive	Deductive thought	Formal stage (age 11 or 12 and beyond)	To teach deductive method of inquiry (hypothesis formation and experimentation)
Transductive	Artistic or transductive	Transductive thought	Concrete or formal stage (ages 8 and beyond)	To teach artistic methods of inquiry (use of pattern, form, theme, repetition)

Self-Evaluation of Learning

The second part of this book has dealt with the objectives, the pedagogical principles, and the alternative types of discovery lessons. You may want to check your understanding of this section by completing the following exercises and comparing your answers to the answers provided on page 236.

Directions: Below a sample lesson plan is presented. Read the plan, then answer the following questions:

1. What type of discovery lesson is this? (Open inductive, structured inductive, simple deductive, semideductive, hypotheticodeductive, or transductive?)
2. What logical structure must children use in order to deal with this lesson? (Order, class, number, combinativity, associativity, reversibility, identity, or tautology and iteration?)
3. What values might children develop if the teacher follows procedure #4, described in the lesson plan?

SAMPLE LESSON PLAN

OBJECTIVES FOR PUPILS

1. Pupils will generalize from given data
2. Pupils will apply the generalization to new examples
3. Pupils will state the generalization: if $A = B$ and $B = C$, then $A = C$.

MATERIALS

A worksheet for pupils, to be supplemented by additional data recorded on the board, or in the form of concrete materials organized on tables around the room. The worksheet would be as follows:

Directions: All of the problems below are really the same problem. Some
of them are already done correctly. The rest need to be completed. If you are not sure how to complete them, study those
that have already been completed.   ∴ means therefore.

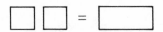

□ □ = □   ↑ ↑ ↑ = ↓ ↓ ↓

□ = □   ↓ ↓ ↓ = 0 0 0
        □

∴ ____ = ____   ∴ ↑ ↑ ↑ = 0 0 0

2 pints = 1 quart   12 dozen eggs = 144 eggs
1 quart = 4 cups   144 eggs   = 1 gross of eggs
       =
∴ __ = __   ∴ 12 dozen eggs = 1 gross of eggs

(5¢) (5¢) = (10¢)   (50¢) (50¢) = [$1 (G.W.) $1]

(10¢) = (1¢)(1¢)(1¢)(1¢)(1¢)   [$1 (G.W.) $1] = (25¢)(25¢)
         (1¢)(1¢)(1¢)(1¢)(1¢)   (25¢)(25¢)

∴ _____ = _____   ∴ _____ = _____

4 nickels = 20 pennies   1 nickel = 5 pennies
20 pennies = 2 dimes   5 pennies = ½ dime

∴   4 nickels = 2 dimes   ∴   _____ = _____

3 feet = 1 yard   4/8 = 1/2
1 yard = 36 inches   1/2 = 2/4

∴   3 feet = 36 inches   ∴   _____ = _____

$$2/2 = 3/3$$
$$3/3 = 4/4$$

Joe's score = Maria's score
Maria's score = Pedro's score

∴ ____ = ____

∴ _____ = _____

$$2 + 4 = 5 + 1$$
$$5 + 1 = 3 + 3$$

$$4 + 2 = 2 \times 3$$
$$2 \times 3 = 10 - 4$$

∴ $2 + 4 = 3 + 3$

∴ _____ = _____

$$A = B$$
$$B = C$$

4 quarts = 1 gallon
1 gallon = 8 pints

∴ ____ = ____

∴ 4 quarts = 8 pints

NOTES ON PROCEDURE

1. The younger the children, the more concrete and manipulative this lesson must be. Those children who do not readily see the solution as the lesson is currently written will need to work with the concrete materials in order to see and compare A with B, B with C, and A with C.

2. Many students will not see that the conclusion must include a term from each of the first two statements. They will, for example, conclude that $B = A$ or that $C = B$, deriving, through the use of the commutative property, a statement that stems from one, not two, of the earlier statements. The solution to this is to ask them to compare what they have done with those problems that have been done correctly in the assignment. This often helps them to infer the rules.

3. One may find that, after puzzling over the problems in this lesson, the children remain uncertain as to the solution. The teacher should then put the problems on the board. He should put up one problem that is not completed and next to it one that is completed, describing what he is writing as he does it. He should then add two more problems, one of which hasn't been completed and one of which has been completed. When the five completed problems are on the board next to five noncompleted problems, the teacher should do one of the uncompleted problems and then ask the children to try the next one. The placing of the problems side by side, the verbalizing of what is being put on the board, and the revealing of the problems one at a time should all help the children to see what is called for.

4. If your lesson is still not getting the desired response, observe, "This is a tough problem. We'll leave it here and try it tomorrow. We'll get it."

We have always found this assignment a difficult one to pull off. It takes patience, much data, and a willingness to stand by while the children try all sorts of wild guesses and defy the obvious before them.

EVALUATION

When the children seem to be handling these problems successfully, ask them to draw as many conclusions as they can from the following:

$$A = B$$
$$B = C$$
$$C = D$$

Using all three statements we conclude $A = D$.
Using the first two statements we conclude $A = C$.
Using the last two statements we conclude $B = D$

Discuss this with children. Then try:

$$H = I$$
$$I = P$$
$$P = Q$$
$$Q = R$$

Then discuss.

PART III

A CHALLENGE
TO DO IT YOURSELF

One drawback to teaching by discovery is that elementary school textbooks frequently use another kind of format. While there are many
instructional materials available today which utilize discovery procedures,
a preponderance of the textbooks and workbooks published still follow
prescriptive procedures. The imaginative teacher need not be stymied by
this fact, however. A prescriptive lesson can be transformed into a
discovery lesson by the addition of some data and some carefully worded
questions. This is a skill which any teacher can master rather quickly,
making use of the principles discussed in the foregoing chapters.

Chapters 7 through 13 are designed to help the reader gain skill in
planning discovery lessons to achieve various objectives. We have dealt here
with four of the types of discovery lessons mentioned in Chapter 6: the
semideductive lesson, the structured inductive lesson, the open inductive
lesson, and the transductive lesson. These are the lessons which can be
used most effectively with elementary school children.

The other two types of discovery lesson (the simple deductive and
the hypotheticodeductive) are only useful with children who are in the
formal operations stages, ages eleven or twelve and beyond. We do not
believe that these two types of lessons can be taught very effectively to
many elementary school children, and thus have not dealt with them
here.

In this part the reader will be presented with some suggestions for
use of a particular type of lesson. He will then be asked to plan a lesson
of this type himself. Sample lessons of the same type which have been
"tested in action" are then presented for comparison and analysis.

chapter 7

Organizing Data
for the Semideductive
Discovery Lesson

In a semideductive discovery lesson, the first decision to be made is what concept or generalization is to be taught. The selection of data is not a terribly critical problem, since the deductive system (e.g., mathematical rules) control or limit the possible generalizations.

The teacher, however, can control what reality will be presented, what type of data is presented, the amount of data or reality, the organization of the data or the reality as it is presented, the speed of the presentation, the amount of time the child has to reflect upon the data, the rules by which the child responds to the data, and the generalizations from the data that are treated in detail.

Through these controls the teacher can affect the type of generalization the child arrives at, the specific generalization, the speed of arrival, and the techniques of investigation the child learns. The child is, of course, asking questions of the data in response to the teacher's questions of the data. The teacher's question and the child's question are of different types. The teacher's question asks the child for a statement that describes the data, or a conclusion that follows from the data. To get the answer to the teacher's question, however, the child must answer several prior questions. He asks: How do I proceed? How do I organize the data to yield the appropriate response? What skills do I bring to bear? What method will be most productive? What hypothesis can I construct that might prove useful when tested? It is the pursuit of the answer to the child's questions that causes the significant learning in the activity. The function of the teacher's question is to stimulate the child's questions. The result of the teacher's question is to so engage the child that he learns something of how to ask questions, to hypothesize, to organize data, to test hypotheses, to handle variables in a systematic fashion, to arrive at a "true" statement—true not because the teacher says so, but because it meets the tests the child has constructed, because it responds to the child's questions and the criteria he has developed, because he has followed the rules of the game.

The above is important because all of the child's life he must seek new answers and learn new truths. The answers he will arrive at are a function of how skillfully he can pose questions, handle data, wrestle with the facts, and determine what the facts are. It is only by this process of inquiry that one can avoid "inert knowledge."

The result of a teacher's question ought to be twofold: first, knowledge about the data is arrived at; second, skills in intellectual inquiry are learned.

The first, to be meaningful, must occur in the presence of the second. The mature student needn't, of course, experience intellectual inquiry for every bit of knowledge he arrives at. The mature student knows how historical truth is arrived at and therefore knows a great deal more about a historical statement than the statement alone would seem to reveal. The same holds for statements in the sciences and in other disciplines. Young children of elementary school age are not mature students, however; hence, the teacher's goal is more than teaching knowledge about the data. It is also to teach the child how to deal with the data.

The foregoing principles of instruction follow from the propositions dealing with the role of the teacher which were presented in Chapter 5. These propositions were:

The teacher must determine what concept he wishes the child to learn.
The teacher must determine what reality will yield that concept if the child interacts with reality.
The teacher must endeavor to get the child to interact with reality.
The teacher must endeavor to keep the child interacting until all contradictions between the child's concepts and reality are resolved.

SELECTION OF DATA

What reality one presents to a child is a function of one's ends and of how children learn. To put it another way, the generalizations one wishes to teach must be embedded in the reality presented to the child.

It is not enough, however, that the generalization be embedded in the reality. The child must have the necessary concepts at his disposal to make sense of the reality. Further, he must have the logical structures necessary to rearrange and/or modify his existing concepts.

These principles follow from the propositions dealing with children's relationships to reality which were stated in Chapter 5. Those propositions, you may recall, were:

Elementary school age children have certain logical structures with which they examine reality.

The seven- to eleven-year-old produces knowledge through a process of interacting with reality.

Two conditions may exist vis-à-vis the concepts in the child's mind and the reality with which the child interacts: agreement or contradiction.

When the first condition exists over an extended period of time, boredom results.

When the second condition exists, the child deals with the contradiction by blocking it out or by adapting to the contradiction through assimilation or accommodation.

There are several additional principles to be considered in relation to the selection of data. First, the simultaneous manipulation and observation of reality makes for the best learning situation. Second, if manipulation is not feasible, then observation of reality provides the second-best learning situation. Third, observation of reality is a better learning situation than observation of a representation of reality.

The more complete the interaction between the child and the reality, the better. The more senses used in the interaction, the better. Consequently, manipulation plus observation is more effective than observation alone. Representations of reality are one step removed from the senses, and thus interaction is less complete. For this reason, representations do not provide as good a learning situation as reality itself.

This cluster of principles regarding the selection of data needs to be examined in more detail because the handling of variables related to these principles is what the technical side of teaching is all about.

Perhaps these principles simply state the obvious. From the data selected, the child must be able to move toward the desired facts, concepts, and observations. To offer $2 + 2 =$ and $2 + 3 =$ to a class and expect them to conclude that verbs show tense is patently ridiculous. One must offer verbs. One can, however, often offer, or children may select, a variety of types of data all of which will yield the same generalizations.

FORM OF DATA

We can categorize reality or data into:

a. That which the child can manipulate and observe
b. That which the child can only observe

c. That which is representational, i.e., is pictorial

d. That which is abstract, i.e., is a proposition

While material may be presented to children in any of the four forms suggested above, abstract data should only be given to the child after he has had much experience with the other three types of material. Further experience with manipulative materials is preferable to experience with that which can just be observed, and material which can be observed should come prior to that which is representational. Experiences with all four types of materials is the preferred strategy, in the order suggested.

It is often the case, however, that the material to be studied, as it exists in reality, cannot be brought into the classroom. In such cases the child will have to move out of the classroom, or representational material will have to be used. From the standpoint of learning, there are advantages to studying rattlesnakes in their native habitat. It is probably not advisable to do so. The next best thing would be to study rattlesnakes in a situation where the snakes were safely enclosed and easily observed by the viewer. This, however, presents problems in the care and feeding of snakes which the teacher might prefer not to face. Given these two complications, the best way to study rattlesnakes would be to observe a great many pictures of rattlesnakes in their natural habitat or a movie that depicts the lives and loves of rattlesnakes.

In addition to the fact that the nature of the reality to be studied sometimes limits the type of data or material available, there are other considerations in determining which type of material is to be used. These considerations relate mainly to the teacher's control of the generalizing process. When manipulative materials are used, children tend to get sidetracked from the main task for the first few sessions. Therefore, if the teacher wishes to teach only a few items he does better to present the materials in representational form. We once watched a young teacher try to teach addition to a kindergarten class using washers. The task for the children was to place x number of washers to their left, y number of washers in front of them, $x + y$ washers to the right, and to then read the statement as $x + y = n$. The first two days were rather difficult ones because the children were busy counting washers, arguing as to who had the most washers, stacking washers, etc. By the third day they were familiar enough with the washers that they were willing to attend more assiduously to the tasks the teacher had in mind. More was accomplished in ten minutes in the third lesson than was accomplished in the first hour of the two earlier lessons. This young teacher was right to stick with her washers. The flexibility of washers as opposed to pictures is enormous.

Because washers can be easily manipulated, they ultimately lead to much more individualization, much more exploration on the part of the children, and much more learning. What would have helped our young teacher would have been a period of free play with the washers. This would seem to be a good general rule with most manipulative materials.

The young teacher mentioned above was very discouraged the first two days and very elated on the third day. Her feeling was that a great deal had been learned on the last day but little had been learned the first two days. In fact, two very significant things were being learned the first two days. First, the children were practicing their ability to count, connecting counting and washers together. They were making sure that they could count. We conclude this from the evidence that older children who count well and are confident of their counting ability give little time to counting objects. Second, much of the confusion in the first two days stemmed from the inability of the children to place the washers in the correct positions on their desk. They had to learn that 3 + 4 meant three washers to the left and four to the right and not the other way around, and that the seven washers that were the sum of 3 + 4 had to go to the right of the equal sign. A considerable amount of necessary learning was taking place that the young teacher failed to see—learning that had to do with constructing a number statement and the rules for such construction, as well as additional insights into the concept of equality. In short, they were learning something of the methodology of mathematics.

The teacher can control the propositions to be generalized in two ways. One way is in the selection and presentation of the data, which we shall momentarily discuss in more detail. The other way is in the methods, strategies, rules, and operations he teaches the children to apply to or use with the data. These methods or rules must be taught well if any worthwhile propositions about the data are to be developed by the children.

PACING OF DATA

One of the advantages of the washers in the lesson above was that each child could move at his own pace. The teacher who works at a felt board with the same lesson moves so slowly that most of the children are bored to tears. The teacher who uses washers can put five to ten problems before the class. Each child can move at his own rate, and the teacher is free to move about the room observing who is getting what and who is having difficulty where. The teacher can also ask specific questions of individual youngsters and vary the assignment for individual children. The major advantage from the child's standpoint is that he is wrestling with the problem itself and not passively sitting. The major advantage from the teacher's standpoint is that he knows how each child is doing with each problem, not how one child is doing with one problem.

There is another point to be made here and that has to do with speed and learning. The human mind must have data if it is to produce sound generalizations. In Chapter 2 you saw that the more data you had the better your generalizations and the more confidence you felt in the truth of the generalization. But, it is not enough to have data. One must recognize that the various pieces of data can be related by a generalization —or if not "can be," might be. To do this the pieces of data must be close enough together in time to be connected. If one gets ptomaine poisoning, one looks to what has been eaten recently, not to what has been eaten six months ago. A woman who wishes to indicate that she is deeply offended by a man's actions ought to slap him immediately. If she doesn't say anything for a year and then slaps him she may feel better for it but he will never make the connection between his actions and the slap. Consequently, he will fail to learn that she judged his earlier action to be offensive.

Teachers working at felt boards and chalk boards often move like the woman in our story. They take one minute to establish $1 + 5 = 6$, another minute to establish that $2 + 4 = 6$, yet another to establish that $3 + 3 = 6$, and so on until $4 + 2 = 6$ and $5 + 1 = 6$ and $0 + 6 = 6$ are established. The children are then expected to say that $4 + 2$ equals $2 + 4$ and that $1 + 5$ equals $5 + 1$. Rarely do they see it, unless they already know it. The reason is speed. By the time $6 + 0 = 6$ is established no one remembers anything at all about $1 + 5 = 6$. $1 + 5 = 6$ may still be on the board but it has long since left the child's mind. It is the reverse phenomenon of "out of sight, out of mind." We now have "out of mind, out of sight." The teacher should move the children quickly from one problem to the next if he expects them to see how the problems are related. Manipulative materials will allow children to move at a more effective pace.

While speaking of pace, let us note in passing that the phrase "the child's own pace" may have certain polemic advantages to some educators, but we find it to be largely nonsense. If left *entirely* to their own pace many students would never get anything done.

AVAILABILITY OF DATA

It is true, however, that different children will vary in the length of time they take to get an insight, even though the amount of data available and its organization are identical. Insight sometimes comes very quickly, sometimes slowly. Sometimes we wonder what took us so long to see what is now very obvious. There are several factors operating here. First, the material from which the insight is to be gained must be readily recalled. The manipulative material must remain in the necessary form, work on the board should remain where it can be seen, representational material should remain in the open. We have seen many an experienced teacher work a new process through with the children (perhaps borrowing in subtraction). All too frequently the teacher erases each example after it has been completed and then works through another example, which is in turn erased while a third example is examined. In our view each example should be left so that each child may compare the examples to each other as questions arise in the child's mind. It is much easier to generalize from four examples than from one. Remember: out of sight, out of mind. Further, how does one generalize from one example? Usually, inaccurately. Developing children's skills at generalizing from one example leads to stereotyping and overgeneralization. These are hardly ends we wish to pursue.

If the example is left on the board, at 10:00 a.m. some child's wandering attention may light on the problems, and reexamination of the facts before him may lead to the desired insights. He won't get there if it has all been erased and he has to recall the examples. Indeed, he won't even try. We see, then, that the speed with which the data is presented is very important, as well as the availability of the material and examples beyond the time of their presentation.

AMOUNT OF DATA

Another factor of immense importance is the amount of data presented. One teacher we know was asked for help in long division by a fifth-grade child in another teacher's class. He wrote the following problem down on a large sheet of paper.

$$489/\overline{5673425965043062000095672} \text{ etc.}$$

He then directed the child as follows: "I will do the problem and you will observe. In doing the problem I will make no intentional errors. When you think you know all the steps I'm following observe me a while longer to check your thinking. When you are sure you know what steps I'm following take the pencil from my hand and finish the problem."

Compare this amount of data here with the usual. It's infinite. The teacher or child can keep adding data until it is no longer needed or no longer wanted.

Compare the organization which enables the amount of data to be unlimited and which enables the four steps of long division to be repeated over and over again until the pattern is seen. It is an organization which keeps the speed and pace of data presentation at a uniform rate, subject only to the variations in speed the teacher may wish to introduce.

The amount of data a child receives is as important as any other factor. For years we have talked about "enrichment" for the gifted, while intellectually it is the slow learner that needs more data. We must speed up the flow of data to the child who needs more data. This means more data for the same period of time. More data means more opportunity to generalize. If a class of children who know that numbers that end in 1, 3, 5, 7, and 9 are odd, while those ending in 0, 2, 4, 6, and 8 are even is given the two statements $2 \times 2 = 4$ and $2 \times 3 = 6$, they will be hard put to conclude that an even number times an odd or an even number will yield an even number and that an odd number times an odd number will yield an odd number. Much more data is needed, data that can be organized so that it will yield generalizations like the two above.

ORGANIZATION OF DATA

The presentation of the data or material can be varied in a number of ways. We have already indicated that the form (i.e., manipulative, representational, abstract, etc.) in which the data is presented is one variable. The speed of presentation is a second variable; the amount of data is a third variable; the amount of time the data remains before the child, or its availability, is a fourth variable.

The logical organization of the data and the physical proximity of the different pieces of data are other variables that affect learning. Suppose the end is to have children develop the following generalizations: (1) An odd number times an odd number equals an odd number; (2) An even number times any number (odd or even) yields an even number. A special instance of the above is that 5 times an odd number yields a number ending in 5 and 5 times an even number yields a number ending in zero. Further, suppose we wish to bring children to recognize the commutative property of multiplication. If we offer children a single long list of numbers times other numbers they may not observe any of these regularities. Consider, however, the following organizations of the same data. Look for possible advantages of one organization over the other. (For each of the organizations I–VII, assume the child is given the direction, "Construct a rule relating to odd and even numbers when they are multiplied together.")

Organization I

$4 \times 3 = 12$	$3 \times 7 = 21$
$2 \times 7 = 14$	$5 \times 7 = 35$
$5 \times 6 = 30$	$1 \times 9 = 9$
$8 \times 8 = 64$	$9 \times 7 = 63$
$7 \times 8 = 56$	$3 \times 3 = 9$
$8 \times 3 = 24$	$7 \times 5 = 35$
$6 \times 7 = 42$	$9 \times 3 = 27$
$4 \times 6 = 24$	$3 \times 9 = 27$
$12 \times 3 = 36$	$5 \times 3 = 15$
$3 \times 4 = 12$	$7 \times 3 = 21$
$6 \times 4 = 24$	$7 \times 9 = 63$
$3 \times 8 = 24$	$9 \times 1 = 9$
$6 \times 5 = 30$	$3 \times 5 = 15$
$8 \times 5 = 40$	
$8 \times 7 = 56$	
$7 \times 6 = 42$	
$5 \times 8 = 40$	

Organization II

$4 \times 3 = 12$	$3 \times 7 = 21$
$2 \times 7 = 14$	$5 \times 7 = 35$
$6 \times 5 = 30$	$1 \times 9 = 9$
$8 \times 8 = 64$	$9 \times 7 = 63$
$8 \times 7 = 56$	$3 \times 3 = 9$
$8 \times 3 = 24$	$7 \times 5 = 35$
$6 \times 7 = 42$	$9 \times 3 = 27$
$4 \times 6 = 24$	$3 \times 9 = 27$
$12 \times 3 = 36$	$5 \times 3 = 15$
$4 \times 3 = 12$	$7 \times 3 = 21$
$6 \times 4 = 24$	$7 \times 9 = 63$
$8 \times 5 = 40$	$9 \times 1 = 9$
	$5 \times 3 = 15$

Organization III

$4 \times 3 = 12$	$3 \times 7 = 21$
$3 \times 4 = 12$	$7 \times 3 = 21$
$5 \times 6 = 30$	$5 \times 7 = 35$
$6 \times 5 = 30$	$7 \times 5 = 35$
$8 \times 3 = 24$	$1 \times 9 = 9$
$3 \times 8 = 24$	$9 \times 1 = 9$
$6 \times 7 = 42$	$9 \times 7 = 63$
$7 \times 6 = 42$	$7 \times 9 = 63$
$8 \times 5 = 40$	$9 \times 3 = 27$
$5 \times 8 = 40$	$3 \times 9 = 27$
$4 \times 6 = 24$	$5 \times 3 = 15$
$6 \times 4 = 24$	$3 \times 5 = 15$
$7 \times 8 = 56$	$3 \times 3 = 9$
$8 \times 7 = 56$	
$2 \times 7 = 14$	
$8 \times 8 = 64$	
$12 \times 3 = 36$	

Organization IV

$4 \times 3 = 12$	$3 \times 7 = 21$
$3 \times 4 = 12$	$7 \times 3 = 21$
$8 \times 3 = 24$	$1 \times 9 = 9$
$3 \times 8 = 24$	$9 \times 1 = 9$
$6 \times 7 = 42$	$9 \times 7 = 63$
$7 \times 6 = 42$	$7 \times 9 = 63$
$4 \times 6 = 24$	$9 \times 3 = 27$
$6 \times 4 = 24$	$3 \times 9 = 27$
$7 \times 8 = 56$	$3 \times 3 = 9$
$8 \times 7 = 56$	$a \times b = c$
$2 \times 7 = 14$	$b \times a =$
$7 \times 2 =$	
$8 \times 8 = 64$	
$12 \times 3 = 36$	
$3 \times 12 =$	
$5 \times 6 = 30$	$5 \times 7 = 35$
$6 \times 5 = 30$	$7 \times 5 = 35$
$5 \times 8 = 40$	$3 \times 5 = 15$
$8 \times 5 = 40$	$5 \times 3 = 15$
$5 \times 4 = 20$	$5 \times 9 = 45$
$4 \times 5 = 20$	$9 \times 5 =$

Organization V

4 × 3 = 12	5 × 3 = 15
3 × 7 = 21	5 × 4 = 20
3 × 4 = 12	5 × 5 = 25
7 × 3 = 21	5 × 6 = 30
8 × 3 = 24	5 × 7 = 35
1 × 9 = 9	5 × 8 = 40
6 × 7 = 42	5 × 9 = 45
9 × 7 = 63	5 × 10 = odd or even?
7 × 6 = 42	5 × 11 = odd or even?
7 × 9 = 63	5 × 12 = odd or even?
4 × 6 = 24	5 × 13 = odd or even?
9 × 3 = 27	5 × 14 = odd or even?
6 × 4 = 24	5 × 15 = odd or even?
3 × 9 = 27	5 × 17 = odd or even?
7 × 8 = 56	
3 × 3 = 9	
8 × 7 = 56	

Organization VI

4 × 6 = 24	3 × 7 = 21	7 × 3 = 21	6 × 4 = 24
7 × 8 = 56	8 × 7 = 56	1 × 9 = 9	9 × 1 = 9
6 × 7 = 42	9 × 7 = 63	7 × 6 = 42	7 × 9 = 63
8 × 3 = 24	7 × 5 = 35	5 × 7 = 35	3 × 8 = 24
5 × 3 = 15	3 × 4 = 12	4 × 3 = 12	3 × 5 = 15
8 × 8 = 64	3 × 3 = 9		
E × E =	O × E =	E × O =	O × O =

Organization VII

4 × 6 = 24	3 × 7 = 21	7 × 3 = 21	6 × 4 = 24
8 × 7 = 56	1 × 9 = 9	9 × 1 = 9	7 × 8 = 56
6 × 7 = 42	9 × 7 = 63	7 × 9 = 63	7 × 6 = 42
8 × 3 = 24	7 × 5 = 35	5 × 7 = 35	3 × 8 = 24
4 × 3 = 12	3 × 5 = 15	5 × 3 = 15	3 × 4 = 12
8 × 8 = 64	3 × 3 = 9		

Organization VIII

Fill in the rest of the boxes in this table and answer the questions below.

×	0	1	2	3	4	5	6	7	8	9
0										
1		1		—		—		7		—
2										
3		—		—	12	—		—		—
4				12						
5		—		—		—		—	40	—
6										
7		—		—		35		—		—
8						40				
9		—		—		—		—		—

Questions

What is true of all numbers involved in problems whose answers appear on a line?

What is true of the numbers that appear in the problem whose answers do not appear on a line?

The answers in these latter problems are what kind of numbers?

QUESTIONS TO CONSIDER

Try to answer the following questions before you read further:

In what ways do the eight different organizations of data differ?

What generalizations might children arrive at from each organization?

What organizations require more skill in observation?

ANALYZING ALTERNATIVE ORGANIZATIONS OF DATA

Perhaps the first thing we should observe is that each organization involves use of abstract data; that is, the statements that go to make up the data are propositions. To utilize this type of data efficiently we assume that the children have already some concept of number developed through handling manipulative data, observational data, and representational data. That is to say, they know what evenness, twoness, and threeness are.

Further, they know something about the addition and multiplication processes and have a concept of equivalence. It is further assumed or known that they can recognize that 4,693 is an odd number and that 112 is an even number.

In comparing data organization I to data organization II, we note that in each organization all of the problems in the left-hand column have at least two elements that are even (the answer and one of the left-hand numbers). The chief advantage of organization II is that here the left-hand (or first) element is always even while the left-hand element of the left-hand column in organization I is sometimes odd and sometimes even. The disadvantage of organization II is that children may focus on *merely* the left-hand element of each column and the answer in each column and conclude erroneously that if a multiplication statement *starts* with an even number the answer is even and if it starts with an odd number the answer is odd. The first is, of course, always true. The second may or may not be true. But in organization II there is no evidence to contradict these two statements. Therefore, it may be advantageous to first offer organization II and then follow up with organization I. This would give children an opportunity to revise a generalization on the basis of new evidence, a process which is very important, as Darwin noted (Chapter 5).

The advantage of organization III is that the data is so organized that commutativity may be more easily seen. This can be further enhanced by setting the problems off in pairs as follows:

$$4 \times 3 = 12 \qquad 3 \times 7 = 21$$
$$3 \times 4 = 12 \qquad 7 \times 3 = 21$$

$$5 \times 6 = 30 \qquad 5 \times 7 = 35$$
$$6 \times 5 = 30 \qquad 7 \times 5 = 35$$

$$8 \times 3 = 24 \qquad 1 \times 9 = 9$$
$$3 \times 8 = 24 \qquad 9 \times 1 = 9$$

In organization III, then, the odd-even relationships can be seen as well as the commutativity property of multiplication. However, the special case of multiplying 5 times an odd number or an even number is still buried in the data.

In organization IV we force the five issue to the child's attention by setting the data off physically from the other data but still in the proper columns. In this exercise we introduce another device. By leaving several unanswered problems we may be able to get some insight into the child's understanding of the commutativity problem. The examples with numbers won't necessarily reveal this knowledge but the $a \times b = c$, $b \times a =$ example will. Further, by adding 5×4 and 5×9 we increase the amount of data available to the child. It may turn out that we still do not have enough data (it will for many children) and we shall have to offer more data or to have the children supply more data.

Some teachers prefer to offer the data we have offered but to have the children supply the answer to each problem. We object to this on three grounds. First, it focuses the child's attention on getting the answers to 3×4, 2×7, etc., thus shifting the attention away from odd times odd, even times odd, even times even, and odd times even. Second, if the child makes mistakes, he will have inadequate data. One or two mistakes would be advantageous because the discovery of the generalization would lead to the correction of the mistakes. But a large number of mistakes, careless or otherwise, would be disastrous. Third, the child often takes so long to get the answers down that he has forgotten to look at the statements in terms of odd, even, etc. In short, the speed question enters here.

Organizations V, VI, and VII dispense with the notion of columns of odd times odd equals odd, odd times even equals even, and even times even equals even. Organization V takes four types of statements, odd times odd statements which are commuted to form new statements, and statements involving at least one even number that are also commuted. We do get in the answers column an even, odd, even, odd, . . . pattern that is helpful to the child. Some children may have to rearrange the data in two columns or three or four as the case may be or to label the numbers as odd or even to handle this organization. For fairly sophisticated students who have had experience reorganizing data in order to get the data to yield generalizations this is a good organization.

Organization VI is easier to handle than V because it is laid out in a different perceptual form, which the child who reads finds easier to deal with. The four types of statements (as in organization five, an odd times odds commuted and an even times odd or even commuted) are still randomly arranged. In organization VII the order of the four is held constant. First, an even times an odd or even to yield an even. Second, an odd times odd. Third, the odd times odd commuted and, fourth, the first statement commuted.

Finally, we offer organization VIII to show an organization children are familiar with, to point up how some of the generalizations aimed at may be highlighted, and to show that there are a number of very different ways to organize the data.

CHOOSING AMONG ALTERNATIVES

Given so many alternative organizations, the question arises of which one ought to be used. While a definitive answer to this question cannot be given, there are several things to consider in responding to it. One variable that we have already discussed at some length is what ideas are most easily seen in each organization. Immature students are more likely to see commutativity in organization IV than in organization I. However, not all children are immature students. Some students have learned to explore data for correlations, for patterns, for the unusual. Some students may be in the process of learning to reorganize data in order to see these correlations, patterns, etc. If the focus of the lesson is merely to reveal the commutative property, then organizations III, IV, V, and VI are the better ones to use. If the lesson is aimed at helping children to reorganize data, then organizations I and II are more appropriate because in III, IV, V, and VI the organizing has already been done, while in I and II the data is set down in a rather random fashion.

Another variable is the values the children have learned or are in the process of learning. If the children have come to value quick answers, and prefer answers to the exclusion of process, then organizations I and II may prove too frustrating. If, however, they can tolerate longer periods of not knowing, and can puzzle over how to do things, and can watch their hypothesis fail to bear fruit, then I and II are probably preferable organizations to the children. Here the fun is in the chase and not the final answer.

A teacher who has taught many discovery lessons prior to these lessons will have undoubtedly worked on getting children to value the intellectual processes or rules of the game that yield knowledge. This teacher would expect his students to start with either organization I or II and to produce organizations III, IV, VI, and VII as well as some other organizations. He would further expect that the children would add additional data to rather conclusively show that their generalization held for the whole number system and not just the data available. Indeed, he would expect that they would ask if similar generalizations hold for the operations of addition, subtraction, and division. The one lesson leads, then, to a series of other lessons which are initiated by questions asked by the children and with data selected and organized by the children.

Another consideration, as we hinted above, is that the various organizations are not mutually exclusive. If some children do not see or discover the generalizations we have in mind through examining organization III, we would offer them organization IV to examine in conjunction with organization III. Nor would we hesitate, if the strategy didn't lead to the generalizations, to offer organization VI and then VII or even VIII. We might well vary the means of presentation, offering one organization on ditto sheets, putting another on the board bit by bit, having the child describe the third one out loud, but we shouldn't hesitate to offer all the organizations we had available. Should individual children still fail to see the generalizations, we wouldn't hesitate to let these children discuss with other children what each of them has seen so far. We wouldn't even hesitate at this point to put much of the data on the board, examining out loud as we do so. We would rarely tell them the generalization, however. The major factor governing the decision as to which organization to present first is the sophistication of one's students. The more sophisticated, the less highly organized the data. The less sophisticated, the more highly and carefully organized the data must be.

ASKING QUESTIONS

We need now to look at the matter of teacher questions and student questions. The standard questions of discovery lessons are: What do you observe? Do you see any patterns? What connections do you see? What generalizations can you construct? What hypothesis do you have? The instructions to look for patterns or see if you notice any similarities are generally verbalized early in the lesson. The questions of whether or not the child has a hypothesis or a generalization often remain unasked until the child has demonstrated through his actions that he is indeed operating from one or the other. Children who can answer the last questions in exercises V and VI and $b \times a =$ in exercise IV have a generalization or they would be unable to answer these questions.

Even when the teacher poses a rather pointed question such as, "What generalizations describe what happens when odd and even numbers are multiplied times each other or times themselves?" the question shouldn't be too limiting or constricting. For example, suppose the teacher asks, "Is an odd or an even number the result of multiplying an odd number times an odd number?" To do this moves the child too quickly to the answer and leaves the *children* with little opportunity to frame specific questions.

When posing the general question relating to odd and even numbers the teacher might well leave aside the question of commutativity. If the class knows that the rule is to explore the data from all standpoints, then they will be alert to regularities other than those relating to odd, even, and multiplication. The very specific question yields the quick answer, and consequently, little exploration of data that might lead to other equally productive generalizations. One danger in teacher questioning is that by asking a specific question the teacher tends to steer activity away from all other matters. No question at all is preferable. The command, "Tell me all you can about this data," is the best way. It makes for an indeterminate situation, which is where all inquiry begins. Further, children often discover what teachers didn't know existed.

The more sophisticated the student, the fewer and less specific the questions the teacher need ask. The question here is: How does one move children to being sophisticated students? The answer, we suggested in Chapter 5, lies in two factors. First, children by their nature are willing to pursue almost any indeterminate situation until it is a determinate situation. Second, the value system of the scholar must operate in the classroom. We observed that children generally put value on final answers and speed of answers because that is what teachers reward. What would happen, however, if teachers were to offer the data and then say "Observe," "Organize," "Hypothesize," "What do you think?" and keep out such judgments as right or wrong? What would happen if teachers could be patient while children seek rather than saying, "We must get this done by ten o'clock," if teachers could say to children, "See anything yet? No? Keep looking. You will"? If teachers would treat all observations, those that fit the data and those that don't, the same way, then children would come to value the search as well as the answer.

The student role should always be the same, to search for truth. The teacher's role is to psychologically support the student while he is searching. It matters not how far the child gets in the job of acquiring truth this day, this week, or this month. What matters is that he become a skillful student. When this happens the acquisition of knowledge will come as a by-product of being a student. The fact that millions of children never learn to be students is evidence that not much attention is given to teaching the role of student to children. The argument is that the child is not a student because he has not learned any facts. This is in error. It would be much more accurate to say that the child hasn't learned any facts because he never learned to be a student.

The child must be supported when he asks questions, supported when he pursues and organizes data, supported when he constructs hypotheses, supported when he tests hypotheses, supported when he tries to frame his generalizations with precision, and complimented only a little when he gets the answer. Supportive statements at this point can take the form, "Are you sure? Yes? Okay. Is there anything else in the data?" Too much external reward for achieving the "right" answer will direct children's attention away from the value of the search.

chapter 8

Sample Lessons
of the Semideductive Type

As the walrus in Lewis Carroll's *Through the Looking Glass* said, "The time has come. . . ." We now ask the reader to produce a number of semideductive discovery lessons. Following each assignment, we shall offer the same lesson as we would construct it, for the reader's comparison. In most instances ours are lessons which we have taught successfully to children in elementary school. Your lesson and ours may come out pretty much the same or they may differ considerably in selection, presentation, organization, and amount of data. The means of testing may also differ. We should, however, each have a lesson that is consistent with the theory of discovery laid out in the preceding chapters.

Before setting out the lessons to be designed it may be helpful to list the questions we ask ourselves as we develop a discovery lesson. We proceed with the following questions:

1. What propositions do we wish the children to induce from this lesson and/or what procedures do we wish to have the children learn?
2. What strategies should we employ so that the children can see or infer the necessary procedures and handle them effectively?
3. What data are necessary to induce the propositions we wish to teach?
4. What presentation of the data will enhance the child's chances of making the right connection?
   a. What should our order of presentation be?
   b. What logical organization should we give the data?
   c. What physical organization should we give the data?
   d. With what speed should the data be presented?
   e. What form should the data take? (Manipulative, representative, or symbolic?)

  f. What questions should we ask of the data?

  g. What alternative presentations of the data should we have ready?

  h. What alternative data should we have ready?

5. What performance on the part of the children will we accept as evidence that they have generalized the proposition?

6. What data can we offer in a disguised form to test children's understanding of the proposition?

With these questions and a careful examination of previous lessons described in Chapters 6 and 7, the reader should be well equipped to plan a series of discovery lessons on his own.

A total of four assignments are made in this chapter. It is not necessary for you to complete each assignment. But we do urge you to go through the process of planning at least one lesson *before* you read the lessons we have constructed.

ASSIGNMENT I

  Construct a discovery lesson that will lead children to induce the proposition that addition and multiplication are commutative while subtraction and division are not. Assume some ability on the part of the children to add, subtract, multiply, and divide.

SAMPLE LESSON I

PROPOSITIONS TO BE INDUCED

The operations of addition and multiplication are commutative. The operations of subtraction and division are not.

STRATEGIES TO BE EMPLOYED

Presentation of data
Children's organization of data
Teacher questions and/or student discussion of data

PRESENTATION OF DATA

  Below are thirty-two true mathematical statements. Regroup these statements by operations. In the statements = stands for "is equal to" and ≠ stands for "is *not* equal to." Demonstrate that each statement is true.

$2 + 4 = 4 + 2$

$13 - 7 \neq 7 - 13$

$12 \div 4 \neq 4 \div 12$

$8 \times 4 = 4 \times 8$

$3 + 5 = 5 + 3$

$100 \div 10 \neq 10 \div 100$

$20 - 10 \neq 10 - 20$

$100 \times 50 = 50 \times 100$

$114 - 100 \neq 100 - 114$

$6 \div 2 \neq 2 \div 6$

$96 + 27 = 27 + 96$

$20 \times 2 = 2 \times 20$

$50 \times 16 = 16 \times 50$

$7 \times 8 = 8 \times 7$

$9 - 2 \neq 2 - 9$

$4 - 2 \neq 2 - 4$

$6 + 9 = 9 + 6$

$\dfrac{1}{4} \div \dfrac{1}{2} \neq \dfrac{1}{2} \div \dfrac{1}{4}$

$100 + 50 = 50 + 100$

$13 + 27 = 27 + 13$

$300 \div 100 \neq 100 \div 300$

$14 - 9 \neq 9 - 14$

$16 \div 8 \neq 8 \div 16$

$16 + 94 = 94 + 16$

$100 \div 50 \neq 50 \div 100$

$6 \times 9 = 9 \times 6$

$16 - 94 \neq 94 - 16$

$3,000 \times 2 = 2 \times 3,000$

$17 + 3 = 3 + 17$

$24 \div 6 \neq 6 \div 24$

$12 \times 10 = 10 \times 12$

$100 - 150 \neq 150 - 100$

The reorganized data will appear roughly as follows:

$2 + 4 = 4 + 2$

$3 + 5 = 5 + 3$

$6 + 9 = 9 + 6$

$100 + 5 = 5 + 100$

$13 + 27 = 27 + 13$

$16 + 94 = 94 + 16$

$96 + 27 = 27 + 96$

$17 + 3 = 3 + 17$

$8 \times 4 = 4 \times 8$

$100 \times 50 = 50 \times 100$

$20 \times 2 = 2 \times 20$

$50 \times 16 = 16 \times 50$

$7 \times 8 = 8 \times 7$

$6 \times 9 = 9 \times 6$

$3,000 \times 2 = 2 \times 3,000$

$12 \times 10 = 10 \times 12$

$13 - 7 \neq 7 - 13$

$20 - 10 \neq 10 - 20$

$114 - 100 \neq 100 - 114$

$14 - 9 \neq 9 - 14$

$9 - 2 \neq 2 - 9$

$4 - 2 \neq 2 - 4$

$16 - 94 \neq 94 - 16$

$100 - 150 \neq 150 - 100$

$12 \div 4 \neq 4 \div 12$

$100 \div 10 \neq 10 \div 100$

$\frac{1}{4} \div \frac{1}{2} \neq \frac{1}{2} \div \frac{1}{4}$

$300 \div 100 \neq 100 \div 300$

$16 \div 8 \neq 8 \div 16$

$100 \div 50 \neq 50 \div 100$

$6 \div 2 \neq 2 \div 16$

$24 \div 6 \neq 6 \div 24$

Once the data has been reorganized and the truth of all thirty-two statements has been established, children can be asked to add additional examples to any of the four sets of data. They can be asked to note whether these examples follow the pattern for that set. A discussion of the data should lead to the desired generalization. It may also lead to others which can be tested further.

RELATIONSHIP OF THE LESSON
TO THE SEMIDEDUCTIVE MODEL

In this lesson children are thinking inductively, though they are working in a deductive system. As is typical in semideductive lessons, the major objective is to teach subject matter. In this case the focus is on the property of commutativity.

The teacher selects the initial data for this lesson, then asks the children to add additional data. This can be done with a great deal of assurance that the added data, no matter what examples are selected, *will* fit the established patterns.

Children are asked to reorganize the data according to operations. This is a simple criterion and is easily followed. The teacher can be quite sure that the children will all end up with the same groups.

This security in predicting that student responses will follow particular patterns results from the fact that mathematics is a deductive system.

Note that quite a bit of data is provided, and that more can be added by the children. There should be sufficient data for all children to reach a generalization. Note also that children's attention is not focused on getting the answer to each mathematical problem. They begin by looking at operations, and the process of reorganizing data forces them to note the equality or lack of equality in each mathematical statement. Only then do they verify that their data is accurate, testing whether each statement is true. This keeps the testing process from interfering with the pacing of data.

In conducting this lesson the teacher will need to remember to keep the data available to the children. Each child may have his own worksheet to record the reorganized data. Examples added by the children can be recorded on the board as well as on individual worksheets.

It will also be important for the teacher to support the generalizations which children advance and to let these generalizations be tested by the data available rather than by the authority of the teacher.

QUESTIONS TO CONSIDER

In what ways did your lesson fit the semideductive model?

What techniques or strategies were you able to apply in planning this lesson?

ASSIGNMENT II

Construct a discovery lesson that will enable children to induce that if A is greater than B and B is greater than C, then A is greater than C.

SAMPLE LESSON II

PRESENTATION OF DATA

EXERCISE 1

Below are three groups. Each group has three items. Your task is to compare these items.

The criterion we shall use to compare items in group I is length.
The criterion we shall use to compare items in group II is size.
The criterion we shall use to compare items in group III is darkness.

Group I	*Group II*	*Group III*

Are the following statements true? Check yes or no in the appropriate place. Complete unfinished statements so that they are also true, and do not repeat a statement already made.

	yes	no			yes	no
1. B is longer than A.	—	—	10. D is smaller than E.		—	—
2. C is longer than B.	—	—	11. E is smaller than F.		—	—
3. ∴ C is longer than A.	—	—	12. ∴ D is smaller than F.		—	—
4. A is shorter than B.	—	—	13. K is darker than J.		—	—
5. B is shorter than C.	—	—	14. J is darker than H.		—	—
6. ∴ A is shorter than C.	—	—	15. ∴ ___ is darker than ___.		—	—
7. E is bigger than D.	—	—	16. H is not as dark as J.		—	—
8. F is bigger than E.	—	—	17. J is not as dark as K.		—	—
9. ∴ ___ is bigger than ___.	—	—	18. ∴ ___ is not as dark as ___.		—	

EXERCISE 2

The first two statements in each group of three statements below are true statements. Using this knowledge, complete the third statement but do not repeat either of the first two statements as your third statement.

19. New York City has more people than Chicago.

20. Chicago has more people than San Francisco.
21. ∴ New York City has more people than San Francisco.

22. San Francisco has less people than Chicago.
23. Chicago has less people than New York City.
24. ∴ _____ has less people than _____ .

25. San Francisco is warmer than Seattle.
26. Seattle is warmer than Fairbanks.
27. ∴ San Francisco is warmer than Fairbanks.

28. Fairbanks is colder than Seattle.
29. Seattle is colder than San Francisco.
30. ∴ Fairbanks is colder than San Francisco.

31. The Mississippi River is longer than the Colorado River.
32. The Colorado River is longer than the Hudson River.
33. ∴ The _____ River is longer than the _____ River.

34. The Connecticut River is shorter than the Colorado River.
35. The Colorado River is shorter than the Mississippi River.
36. ∴ The _____ River is shorter than the _____ River.

37. Grandmother is older than Mother.
38. Mother is older than I.
39. ∴ _____ is older than _____ .

40. $X > B$
41. $B > F$
42. ∴ ___ > ___

43. p is zittier than r.
44. r is zittier than s.
45. ∴ _____ .

RELATIONSHIP OF THE LESSON
TO THE SEMIDEDUCTIVE MODEL

While a syllogism is a deductive exercise, children are asked to arrive at the rules for constructing relational statements in an inductive manner. They must observe a number of completed statements and figure out the process that was used to complete them.

The variety of data used makes it obvious that selection of data is not a problem in this lesson. The major thing to consider is the concreteness of data in relation to the age of the children.

An important technique to note in this lesson is the strategy of providing some completed statements and some uncompleted statements.

The uncompleted statements serve several purposes. They provide children with a well-defined goal for the lesson. They provide children with an opportunity to test a hypothesis or generalization without verbalizing it. They provide the teacher with feedback as to what children are able to apply a generalization. When completed, these uncompleted statements become additional data for use by children who have not yet achieved a generalization.

Another useful technique shown here is the inclusion of "nonsense" examples to be completed. The problem "*p* is zittier than *r*, *r* is zittier than *s* . . ." is an example. These nonsense statements are useful for teacher evaluation. The child can only complete these statements if he truly understands the generalization. Other kinds of knowledge are not useful to him since the statements lack experiential meaning.

Use of nonsense statements has other benefits as well. They can provide a bit of humor in the lesson. Children may go on to devise their own nonsense statements, for most of them enjoy this kind of playing with language. Also, the correct solution of these types of statements seems to be particularly enhancing to the child's self-concept. He demonstrates to himself that he can solve problems that are really unique.

QUESTIONS TO CONSIDER
    In what ways did your lesson follow the semideductive model?
    What techniques were you able to apply in planning this lesson?

ASSIGNMENT III
    Construct a discovery lesson that will enable children to develop the following generalizations:
        A rectangle has four sides.
        Opposite sides of a rectangle are equal.
        Squares make up a subset of the class of events called rectangles.
        Assume children know very little about squares, triangles, rectangles, etc.

SAMPLE LESSON III

PROPOSITIONS TO BE INDUCED

1. A rectangle has four sides.
2. Opposite sides of a rectangle are equal.
3. Squares make up a subset of the class of events called rectangles.

STRATEGIES TO BE EMPLOYED

Presentation of data that will enable children through organizing data
to classify angles as obtuse, acute, or right angles.

Children group lines according to equal lengths.

Presentation of concrete materials of various shapes.

Children organize data or materials into similar groups using type of
angle and equality of length of sides as criteria.

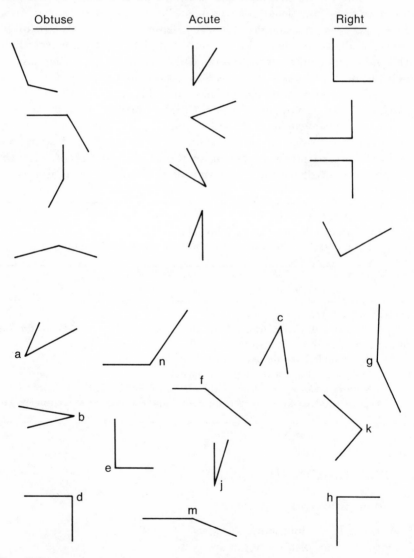

Fig. 8–1

PRESENTATION OF DATA

In Fig. 8–1 there are three columns. Each one has a label at the top and each has four figures, or angles. Below the columns are twelve more figures, or angles, each labeled with a letter. Decide which of the three columns each angle belongs in. Place the letter for the angle in the column that has similar angles.

STRATEGY 2

Evaluate by having children identify various types of angles about the room.

STRATEGY 3

Ask students to measure the lines in Fig. 8–2 and to group all lines of equal length together.

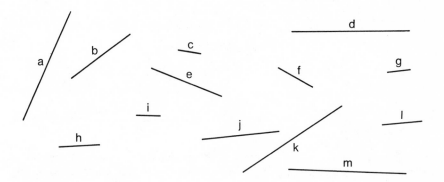

Fig. 8–2

STRATEGY 4

Evaluate by observing whether the task of grouping lines by length is successfully completed by each child.

STRATEGY 5

Give each child a large number of cutouts of which the ones in Fig. 8–3 are typical examples. Offer many similar shapes but few, if any, identical sizes. Instruct the children to group the objects according to similarities they perceive.

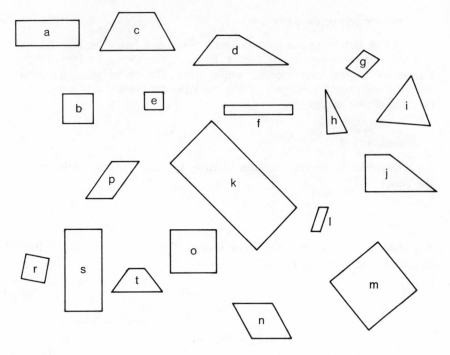

Fig. 8–3

STRATEGY 6

Describe what the members in each of your groups have in common. For example, each figure of one group will have two obtuse angles, two acute angles, two opposite sides that are equal in length, and two opposite sides that are not equal in length. Discuss your findings with your classmates.

STRATEGY 7

Give children the names for the figures in each group—i.e., square, rectangle, etc.

Note: The teacher can include in strategy 5 (Fig. 8–3) a great many triangles and induce some propositions about triangles.

STRATEGY 8

Evaluate by having children construct their own cutouts to fit each group. Can they construct cutouts which do not fit into any of their groups?

RELATIONSHIP OF THE LESSON
TO THE SEMIDEDUCTIVE MODEL

In this lesson children's awareness of geometric concepts such as angle and line is developed gradually, then applied to the organization of concrete geometric forms. Once children have learned to observe such characteristics as type of angle and length of line, they can be left free to organize the concrete data into groups, and to describe the characteristics of their groups. The possible groupings they may devise is limited by the system in which they are operating, so the probability is fairly high that they will group in predictable ways. This is desirable in a lesson that aims at developing specific geometric concepts.

If the teacher were interested in more divergent responses to the materials, he would not structure the children's perceptions through previous experiences. The lesson could then become an open inductive lesson. Strategies for this type of lesson will be discussed in Chapter 11.

In this lesson we have introduced the evaluation strategy of having children produce nonexamples. This provides an additional measure of their understanding of the defining characteristics of each group. It is generally more difficult to produce nonexamples for a particular group than it is to produce examples. Nonexamples here might include circles, pentagons, octagons, etc.

QUESTIONS TO CONSIDER

What techniques did you use in your lesson to direct children's observation to the "criterial attributes" of squares and rectangles?

Did you make use of concrete materials in your plans for this lesson? What advantages or disadvantages might this entail?

ASSIGNMENT IV

Construct a discovery lesson to help children induce the scientific principle that categorization of things may need to be based on more than superficial observation—i.e., things which look alike are not necessarily similar in other characteristics, and things which look different may be similar.

SAMPLE LESSON IV

PROPOSITIONS TO BE INDUCED

Things which look alike are not necessarily alike in other characteristics.
Things which look different may be alike in other characteristics.
Scientific observation involves various techniques besides "just looking."

Lead children to overgeneralize on the basis of superficial observation of data.

Have them correct their generalization on the basis of additional observation of data.

Ask children to give examples of things which look alike. Raise the questions: Are any of these really different? and How could a difference be observed?

Lead into experiments with items which look different.

PRESENTATION OF DATA

Four identical-looking cookie boxes are placed on a table at the front of the room, along with two identical-looking boxes of cereal and three identical-looking bags of candy. The items are arranged in random order. Children are asked to look at them and decide how they would group these items, putting things that are alike together.

Several children are asked to report their grouping to the class. It is expected that all (or nearly all) will agree on the obvious three groups of items.

One child is asked to come to the front of the room and rearrange the items according to the agreed-upon grouping. In handling the cereal boxes, this child will probably note that they are not the same weight (one is full and one is empty). Several children may be asked to apply the test of lifting the two cereal boxes in order to decide whether they are really the same.

Next the teacher may ask the children whether they want to test their grouping of the cookie boxes further. He might ask: How can we decide whether these four boxes are really alike? . . . If they look the same and feel the same, does that mean they are the same? . . . How can we be sure?

Someone will probably suggest opening the boxes to look inside. When this suggestion is followed the children will see that one of the boxes contains chocolate chip cookies while the other three contain oatmeal cookies. (It is not necessary for the teacher to eat a whole box of oatmeal cookies in order to perform this substitution prior to the lesson.)

The children will undoubtedly decide that the bags of candy need testing, too. Since the candy inside all three bags looks alike—e.g., they are all "M and M's"—the class may decide that an important final test will be to eat a piece of candy from each of the three bags to see if they taste alike. This test had best be carried out by all members of the class.

Children can now be asked to revise their earlier grouping of items, on the basis of their additional information. The teacher can ask them to indicate the kinds of observation they used to gather information about the items and whether they can think of other ways of observing. Their suggestions can be recorded on the board.

Finally, children can be asked to give examples of things which are fairly similar in appearance, but which may be different in other ways. They may respond initially by mentioning living things. Young children may include things like worms and caterpillars in their list. These must be observed over a period of time to note physical changes (e.g., a caterpillar spins a cocoon). Older children will include items like dolphins and sharks. One way of observing differences between these two animals is to "open them up," like the cookie boxes, and study their insides.

At this point (immediately or in a follow-up lesson) children may be presented with a bizarre assortment of physical objects and be asked to observe them in as many ways as possible, to decide how they are similar to or different from each other. Observations might include:

How much does each item weigh?
How does each item react to a magnet?
What happens when you put each item in a bowl of water?
What happens when you try to bend each item?
What happens if you heat each item?

On the basis of each of these types of observations, children could categorize the items. They might work in groups, each group being responsible for a different type of observation. Children should be able to add other types of observation to the list above.

When their observations and categorizations are completed, children should be able to state the principle that items which look different may have other qualities in common.

RELATIONSHIP OF THE LESSON
TO THE SEMIDEDUCTIVE MODEL

The introduction to this lesson is rather "off-beat," because the data provided does not really "belong" within the deductive system being investigated. To make a compelling point, data is manufactured.

The latter part of the lesson is more typical. Children can be left relatively free to select their own data and their own method of observation. The teacher can be fairly certain that the materials used will respond in predictable ways, according to the laws of physics. On the basis of these reactions, children can readily group the items.

QUESTIONS TO CONSIDER

Were you able to construct a lesson which involved both manipulation and observation of data?

Why would this be particularly important in this lesson?

chapter 9

Strategies for
the Structured Inductive Lesson

To teach a child to think is to move him more and more toward independence, and while no scholar ever becomes completely independent, good scholars do in fact have a self-generating mechanism and an ability to sustain solitary activity over a fairly long period of time.

To be self-generating, however, requires certain values and knowledge of the problem. To sustain an activity again calls for certain values and knowledge. The child doesn't have the values or the knowledge necessary to pull it off. He is other-directed, not inner-directed, when it comes to scholarship, in that his curiosity is diffused. He must be taught to recognize a problem; he must be taught how to attack a problem, how to determine what is relevant, what is factual, what must be organized how, and what questions must be asked. He must learn how to determine what knowledge is of most worth. He must learn to value the whole activity of thinking and to understand why sound thinking is preferable to non-thinking or what Bartlett calls "everyday thinking."[1]

It is precisely because of the above that we need teachers. If the child could already do these things, he wouldn't need a teacher. The reason teaching in a graduate school is so easy is that there is little need for teaching. The early elementary school is where the teacher must know how to teach. His students are very dependent because they have relatively little knowledge of scholarship, its values, or the role of the scholar when compared with the student in a grade school. (We may

[1] Sir Frederick Bartlett, *Thinking: An Experimental and Social Study* (London: George Allen and Unwin, 1958).

be giving some graduate students the benefit of the doubt in assuming that they do know these things.)

We make the above points in order to suggest that learning to be a student is learning to become more and more independent in matters relating to the search for truth. It follows then that teaching is moving to less and less control of the variables involved. The schools of America cannot make a very compelling argument that they are teaching students to think independently when the high school teacher controls every assignment in all details and the colleges offer master's degree courses with 150 students in a lecture room.

In Chapter 7 we offered a fairly detailed analysis of the advantages or the consequences of different organizations in a semideductive discovery lesson. We suggested that which organization one selects to present to a class is a function of several factors, particularly the level of inquiry skills of the children and the knowledge and value objectives of the teacher.

One of the characteristics of the structured inductive discovery lesson is the importance of organization of data. Since attainment of a particular concept is desired, and the system or subject area being dealt with is an inductive one, where varied perceptions or interpretations are quite possible, the teacher may not have as many options regarding organization of data. In this chapter we shall deal with some details of organization and presentation in structured inductive discovery lessons.

TEACHING LONG AND SHORT VOWELS

Many teachers realize that a generalization that can be applied by the children is of inestimable value and, consequently, they strive to teach such generalizations in even the most mundane areas. Such a generalization relates to one-syllable words of the class that includes "fate," "late," "make," "like," "cede," "coke," etc. This lesson has two edges in that it is hoped that the child upon hearing "fat" and "fate" can spell them both correctly with the certain knowledge that "fate" has the *e* and not "fat." The second edge of this lesson is the hope that the child, upon seeing "fat" and "fate," perhaps for the first time, will recognize that the *a* in "fat" is short because it is a single vowel in a one-syllable word and that the *a* in "fate" is long because of the *e* on the end.

Given these ends, the next question concerns what data is needed and available, from which the desired generalizations may be drawn. The following data would seem to meet our needs:

hat	hate	dim	dime	met	mete	dot	dote
fat	fate	fin	fine	pet	Pete	not	note
mat	mate	win	wine			rot	rote
rat	rate	din	dine			tot	tote
pal	pale	twin	twine				
plan	plane	pin	pine				
pan	pane	strip	stripe				
tap	tape	rip	ripe				
bath	bathe	kit	kite				
past	paste	hid	hide				
sat	sate	Sid	side				
		shin	shine				
		bit	bite				
		writ	write				

The data we have so far is written. The sounds are not present. If the children can read the words, they can, of course, supply the sounds. But if they can read all of the words without difficulty, the fact that they can read (i.e., give the correct sound for) "stripe," "paste," "cede," "rote," "tote," "sate," "writ," and "twine" would suggest that they already know one of the generalizations and the teacher need only test whether they can spell these words upon hearing them. If the above is the case, the teacher may wish to go ahead with the lesson with the end in mind of having the children produce written generalizations that describe all of the data.

In most primary classrooms there will be some children who can read all of the words, others who can read some of them, and perhaps some who can read few, if any of them. For these last two groups the sound data must be given to the class. It is clear that to offer all of the written data to the children at one time on ditto sheets and to offer the sound to the children at the same time is an impossibility. One can, however, proceed as follows and accomplish all of one's ends:

Teacher: The word I'm writing is "hat." (*Writes "hat."*) What is it?

Class: "Hat."

T: The word I'm now writing is "hate." (*Writes "hate" while saying this and points out that they look alike but have one difference in looks and one in sound.*) Okay, we have "hat" here (*points*) and "hate" here (*points*). Below "hat" we write "rat" and below "hate" we write "rate." Read these four words as I point to them:

hat   hate

rat   rate

If the class has many poor readers, the teacher should repeat the pointing, having the children read the words aloud until they are fairly sure of which sound goes with what words.

Add "mat" giving the sound for it and then add "mate" giving its sound. Have children read:

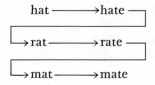

Then have them read them in the following order.

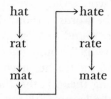

If the children are having some difficulty, have them listen while you read and point or have them listen while you point and a child reads. Then have them read again in the order suggested above. If they are getting it better at this point, reverse the above and go "hate," "hat," "rate," "rat," "mate," "mat."

Then say to the children while pointing, "Here is—

hat   hate

rat   rate

mat   mate

sat   ———

—and what do you think goes here?"

The teacher should give the children time to reflect here and not jump at the first hand that goes up. This is a moment of truth in the lesson, a point where payoff is coming or not coming, a point where the teacher finds out if the strategy has as yet succeeded. If the first hand raised is immediately called upon and the child in question offers a correct answer, all thinking will come to a halt.

One way to handle the situation is to move about the room having children whisper the answer in your ear if they have the sound or show you the written answer on a piece of paper. If they whisper the answer, the teacher then asks, "Can you write it?" If they write the answer, the teacher asks, "Can you say it?" By using this technique the teacher gets more feedback from the class that will tell him who is getting the idea and who isn't.

The use of "sate" here has the advantage of not being a "sight" word. It therefore must be arrived at by means other than recall.

At this point we have on the board:

hat	hate
rat	rate
mat	mate
sat	

It is not necessary to fill in "sate." Those who have it will fill it in mentally. Those who do not will get it later. The teacher then adds "tap" to the left-hand column and "tape" to the right-hand column, reading each word aloud as he does so. Then "plan" and "plane" are added in the same manner. Then "pan" is added to the left-hand column and the children are asked what goes in the right-hand column.

If a good many children are having difficulty, the teacher can go over the words, pointing and reading in the manner suggested above, first moving "hat," "hate," "rat," "rate," "mat," "mate," etc. then moving down one column and then the other, leaving a brief time gap for the nonwritten words in each list.

The teacher can now begin to vary his presentation in a number of ways. He may add "past" and "paste," adding "paste" to the right-hand column first and then "past" to the left-hand column. He may then add "fate" to the right-hand column, reading it as he does so, and ask what goes in the left-hand column. He can then introduce "dim," "dime," "fin," "fine," "win," and a blank.

The lists now are as follows:

hat	hate
mat	rate
rat	mate
sat	
tap	tape
plan	plane
pan	

past	paste
	fate
dim	dime
fin	fine
win	
	sine
	twine
pin	

"Bit," "bite," "hid," "hide," "writ," and "write" may be added now, giving one or the other or both. Then "not" can be offered and the class can try to figure out what goes in the right-hand column. One or two other combinations can then be given. The teacher, however, should not put all of the data on the board but should ask the children if they can think of any pairs of words that fit the two lists.

The above strategy accomplishes two things. First, it serves to test if the generalization has been gotten by any of the students. If students are offering new pairs of words correctly, then it is often reasonable to infer that they have a working knowledge of the generalization. The child that adds "trip" and "tripe" and spells them both correctly probably has the idea. Second, as some children add new data the child who has not yet gotten the generalization will have more data to observe.

Before leaving this lesson several points need to be noted. The child who gets to the point where he can produce new pairs and can apply the rules to nonwords—such as "hap" yields "hape" and "sip" yields "sipe" —should now be required to state the generalization. The stating of the generalization is, of course, a different task than arriving at it and applying it. Teachers have a tendency to accept generalizations from children when only a small part of the necessary conditions are stated. "An even number is a number divisible by two" is incorrect. "An even number is a number divisible by two and having an answer with no remainder" is a much more satisfactory answer. To assist the child to write accurate generalizations the teacher must not read things into the answer. The teacher must demonstrate to the child the consequences of his generalization by offering data consistent with the child's generalization but contradictory to it. For example, the child may state that "one-syllable words have the short vowel sound unless they end in *e*, in which case the first vowel sound is long and the *e* is silent." At this point the teacher should offer the word "beat," which has one syllable with a long vowel sound and does not end in *e*.

The teacher wants eventually to bring the child to the point where the *child* looks for evidence that goes contrary to his generalization. It is obligatory for the thinker not only to try to prove his generalizations but to try to disprove them as well. This is the difference between being a propagandist and a thinker. Often the child will produce a generalization that describes a wide range of data but one or two facts will stand in contradiction. Teachers then like to observe that this is the exception that proves the rule. Unfortunately, few teachers and fewer children know that when this saying originated, to "prove" a rule meant to "test" it. The exception does indeed *test* the rule, and suggests that the rule or generalization needs revision. If we insist that no exceptions are allowed (i.e., that an exception to a proposition means by definition that the proposition fails to meet the test of being a valid generalization), the child will be forced to rework his proposition, to reexamine his data, to try new approaches. It is in reworking, reexamining, and trying new approaches that the child learns. He learns first, what the data is all about, and second, how to think. The acceptance by teachers of half-baked truths doesn't help the child to learn to be anything but a half-baked thinker with a lot of half-baked ideas.

chapter **10**

Sample Lessons of
the Structured Inductive Type

Planning a structured inductive lesson will require a bit more skill on the part of the teacher than planning a semideductive lesson. He must be alert to the possibility that data can be perceived from more than one perspective, and that different interpretations can lead to different generalizations. The goal of a structured inductive discovery lesson is to have children develop a particular concept or generalization within a reasonable length of time (not necessarily within the space of a single lesson). To achieve this goal the teacher must select and organize the data to be presented carefully. As children become more adept at inductive discovery, the teacher will want them to develop more and more independence. One of the skills they will have to develop is the skill of organizing data themselves. The lessons in this chapter require different levels of organizing skills on the part of the children.

In this chapter you will be given six different assignments for lessons to be planned. After each assignment a sample lesson plan to fulfill that assignment, as we would teach it, will be presented. You may select any one assignment from among the six. We strongly urge that you plan your own lesson before you read the sample lesson we present. Of course, your lesson may differ from our lesson. There is more than one way of teaching any concept.

All of our lessons have been taught successfully to elementary school children. You may want to try teaching one of them to your own class, in order to try out some of the strategies suggested in the preceding chapter, Chapter 9.

ASSIGNMENT I

Take a spelling list from any grade level and construct several lessons that will enable children to induce some spelling rules which they can use as a means to improving their spelling. You will need to add additional words (data) to the list. Assume some reading ability (e.g., third-grade reading level—whatever that means).

SAMPLE LESSON I

There are a wide variety of lessons that can be developed here. We included this assignment because it enables us to deal with a problem that many teachers face when they wish to be innovative and try a new teaching method. The problem is that the textbooks that the school requires the teacher to use call for a pedagogy—or a nonpedagogy—that is at odds with the pedagogy the teacher wishes to employ. Usually, however, there is a way around the problem. Most school districts want the material covered. Some even want it learned. The teacher who can accomplish the second will be allowed a great deal of freedom in how he does it.

The typical speller offers twenty words a week, a pretest, some use of the words in sentences, some memorization drill, another pretest, some writing of the words, and a final test. Six weeks later there is a big test. If any of the twenty words each week are related through spelling rules, it is accidental. The solution rests in ignoring the weekly lesson and going directly to the back of the book where all of the words are listed and reorganizing the list by rules. (There are some spelling series on the market which have already been organized in this way.[1])

MATERIALS

Following are some words taken from a speller with some additional words added. They are organized randomly.

Directions: Organize the words below [*see Fig. 10–1*] into eight groups according to vowel sounds.

The final groups should appear as in Fig. 10–2.

[1] The *Basic Goals in Spelling* series by Kottmeyer and Ware (New York: McGraw-Hill Book Company, Webster Division, 1968) is an example of such a series.

letter	seat	gust	wet	cuter
bet	rate	muter	batter	blight
mitt	glider	wide	wake	set
site	fat	brighter	nut	rust
baker	time	lake	mike	putt
fit	taker	mutt	line	hat
vet	mat	better	sight	gnat
dime	flute	let	timer	make
shake	litter	wine	rat	getter
side	flight	sate	strike	glide
sat	butte	fleeter	like	blake
lit	like	hate	cheat	new
net	bale	get	rake	hitter
dine	shut	fleet	wetter	sight
butter	shaker	flake	cat	mete
pat	take	dike	putter	cheat
wetter	setter	mute	met	cake
patter	mutter	pate	bit	sit
meet	jet	slide	light	pet
yet	hit	bright	fatter	matter
fitter	came	feet	sleet	late
mate	meat	bake	liner	sitter
butt	bat	rut	chute	patter
cute	bleat	lime	timer	cheater
diner	like	maker	gate	twine
hater	heat	kite	feat	tame
but	wider	heat	rate	fatter
				later

Fig. 10–1

[ă]	[ĕ]	[ĭ]	[ŭ]
pat	letter	lit	putt
patter	bet	mitt	rust
fat	vet	hit	nut
mat	net	fit	rut
bat	yet	bit	mutt
cat	setter	hitter	shut
rat	jet	sit	gust
hat	better	sitter	putter
gnat	let	litter	mutter
sat	get	fitter	but
matter	wet		butt
fatter	met		butter
batter	set		
	getter		
	pet		
	wetter		

Fig. 10–2

[ā]	[ē]	[ī]	[ū]
shake	heat	site	cute
mate	mete	dime	flute
rate	cheat	side	mute
bale	fleet	dine	muter
take	cheater	diner	chute
came	meat	time	butte
hater	meet	flight	
lake	heat	like	
sate	seat	wider	
hate	feet	wide	
flake	feat	dike	
pate	bleat	slide	
bake	heater	bright	
rate	meter	lime	
wake	fleeter	kite	
shaker		wine	
make		glide	
blake		sight	
late		timer	
maker		blight	
cake		brighter	
later		glider	
baker			
taker			

Fig. 10–2 (Cont.)

PROCEDURES

When children have formed their eight groups of words, have them add five new words to each group.

Pose the following questions to the children:

How did you organize your groups?
What generalizations can you make about English spelling?
Can you find subgroups in your larger groups?
Do these subgroups lead you to new generalizations?

EVALUATION

Long-term evaluation is the best way of judging the effectiveness of this type of lesson. Do children recall their rules well enough to apply them to spelling of new words? Do they begin to look for regularities of English spellings, rather than rely on memorization of words?

RELATIONSHIP OF THE LESSON
TO THE STRUCTURED INDUCTIVE MODEL

In this lesson children are being asked to use inductive thinking in an area where a good deal of complex and conflicting data exists. The teacher selects the data here to insure that conflicting data will not be introduced at too early a stage in the generalizing process. Data is presented randomly, but children are given directions as to how to proceed to organize it.

This lesson could probably be used with children fairly early in their experience with discovery techniques. Advanced skills in organizing data or testing generalizations are not necessary for children to succeed with this lesson.

Some attention is paid to individual differences. Children are given the opportunity to search for subgroups within the eight major groups, but this is not an assigned task. Thus children with different levels of organizing skills can all work at their own level. Different children can produce different numbers of generalizations.

QUESTIONS TO CONSIDER

Did you provide for individual differences in ability to organize data or to form precise generalizations in your lesson?

If not, how might you vary your materials or your procedure to achieve this?

ASSIGNMENT II

Construct a discovery lesson that will enable children to induce the following rules for capitalizing:

1. The first word in each sentence is capitalized.
2. The months of the year are capitalized.
3. Proper nouns are capitalized.
4. The days of the week are capitalized.

SAMPLE LESSON II

OBJECTIVES FOR PUPILS

1. To induce the rules governing capitalization
2. To organize data in logical groupings
3. To identify means of evaluating generalizations formed

MATERIALS

Give each student a copy of the following:

Assume the paragraphs below have no mistakes in punctuation, spelling, or capitalization.
Assume further that there are a set of conventions or rules relating to capitalization and that these rules have been used to write the paragraphs below.
What are the rules used?
What is your evidence?
How can you test further?

There are thirty days in September, April, June, and November. February has twenty-eight days, in three years out of every four. Each of the remaining months has thirty-one days. Each month must have at least four Mondays, four Tuesdays, four Wednesdays and four of every other day. A month may have five Wednesdays. Any month that has five Wednesdays cannot have five Saturdays, or five Sundays. Can you figure out why this is so? If I can, you can.

George Washington and Abraham Lincoln have birthdays in February. Mr. Washington was the first President of the United States and Mr. Lincoln was the last of his party who could speak with intelligence. Mary Jones and Peter Sanchez also have birthdays in February as do Mr. Partnoy, the art teacher, and Miss Williams, the English teacher.

PROCEDURES

Give children the materials and let them begin to work on their own.

After children have been working for a while it may be helpful to ask a few of them to report on their methods of attacking the problem. (Some children may underline all the capitalized words, for example. Others may write them down on another piece of paper and try to group them.)

Different children will proceed at different rates in this exercise. As children complete their written statements of the rules, they can meet in small groups to compare statements and to discuss the evidence they used. The group can suggest ways of testing these generalizations (e.g., look at the capitals in a library book). Individual children can then take the additional data suggested, and test their own generalizations.

EVALUATION

How well are children able to organize the data presented?
How many ways of testing their generalizations can they identify?
How many children try to find additional evidence for generaliza-

tions relating to use of capitals in "President," "United States," and "English," rather than generalize on the basis of one example.

RELATIONSHIP OF THE LESSON
TO THE STRUCTURED INDUCTIVE MODEL

In this lesson children are being asked to form generalizations dealing with the conventions of written English. There is no logical reason why certain letters are capitalized and others not. But the rules being used can be induced from examples of written English.

The teacher has not organized the data for children. It is presented in its natural state, in the context of paragraphs of written English. To handle this lesson children must have developed a certain degree of independence, both in organizing data and in testing their own generalizations.

To further individualize this lesson, and to insure success for the children who may not have developed this degree of independence, the teacher could have another worksheet prepared to distribute to children who needed additional data. This worksheet might provide the data in a more organized form. For example:

Monday	yesterday
Tuesday	today
Wednesday	tomorrow
February	fall
March	winter
April	spring
May	summer
Mary	girl
Bill	boy
Mr. Jones	man

An interesting follow-up lesson for children who handle this one easily would be to give them some examples of poetry and have them extend their rules of capitalization to that form of writing.

QUESTIONS TO CONSIDER

How much independence or ability to organize data did your lesson require?

Would you teach it to children who were just beginning to use discovery techniques or to children who had developed some problem-solving skills already?

ASSIGNMENT III

Construct a discovery lesson that will enable children to develop the rule that *er* is used when comparing two things and *est* is used when comparing three or more things.

SAMPLE LESSON III

OBJECTIVES FOR PUPILS

1. To induce the rule governing use of *er* and *est* in comparative adjectives
2. To apply the rule to new examples
3. To state the rule

MATERIALS

The following worksheet would be distributed to children:

There are nine sentences below. Four of the sentences use *er* on the end of a word. Four of the sentences use *est* on the end of a word. One of the sentences uses *er* incorrectly and one of the sentences uses *est* incorrectly. Correct them by crossing out the incorrect ending and putting in the correct ending. One sentence has two *er*'s and one *est*. It is correct. Along with the other correct sentences, it should give you a clue.

1. Jack is taller than Ed.
2. Peter is older than Bill.
3. Sam is the tallest boy in the class.
4. Isidor is the older boy in the school.
5. Mr. Jones is the richest man in town.
6. Beulah is biggest than Mary.
7. I am smarter than Annie.
8. The rabbit is the quickest of the small fur-bearing animals.
9. I am taller than Edward, and José is taller than me; therefore, José is the tallest of the three of us.

Cross out the incorrect ending.

1. Solomon was the wise (er) (est) of men.
2. Among runners, Carlos is the fast (er) (est).
3. Between you and me, you're smart (er) (est).
4. Of the five girls on the team, Melody was the tall (er) (est), but Jane was tall (er) (est) than Edith, and Edith was tall (er) (est) than Maria. Alice was the short (er) (est) member of the team.

Write a rule that will tell us when to use *er* and when to use *est*.

PROCEDURES

Children can work individually on this worksheet. When everyone has completed the worksheet, a group discussion can be held in which children compare their statements of rules and try as a group to agree on one statement which best fits the data.

An alternative procedure would be to have each student turn in his worksheet as soon as he has completed a statement. The teacher would read the generalization and provide the student with additional data so that he could test his statement and revise it if necessary.

EVALUATION

How complete are the generalizations that the children produce?

How willing are they to revise their generalizations in the face of conflicting data or more complete statements produced by other children?

RELATIONSHIP OF THE LESSON
TO THE STRUCTURED INDUCTIVE MODEL

This lesson points up the importance of having children apply their tentative generalizations before stating them. And it separates the two different processes of arriving at a generalization and stating it accurately.

An additional point of interest here is the use of inaccurate data which the child must correct. It is assumed that the child will be able to identify the two incorrect sentences and revise them, because children know the rules of language usage at an unconscious level long before they become aware of their knowledge. It is a good idea to introduce the child to the procedure of evaluating *data*. Not all of the data that come to us are accurate and it is important that we pay some attention to checking the accuracy of the data prior to forming a generalization. This exercise introduces that process in a simple way. It would need to be emphasized more in later lessons.

QUESTIONS TO CONSIDER

Could your lesson be used for both individualized instruction and group instruction?

Why would such alternative procedures be important?

ASSIGNMENT IV

This lesson calls for some additional imagination on your part. An archeologist digs in the ruins, uncovering layer after layer of artifacts, buildings, etc., and as he goes he uses certain techniques to protect what he is uncovering and to keep from disturbing the object of his study so as not to unnecessarily change the evidence before he can note what it is and where it was located. He takes careful notes and tries to infer from his notes and from the artifacts he has uncovered the facts that would describe the civilization he has uncovered, the events that took place during the civilization's existence, and the sequence of events in time.

Construct a discovery lesson that will give children an appreciation of some of the difficulties that the archeologist faces as he pursues his work.

SAMPLE LESSON IV

This is a lesson to be used with a boy or girl who has an interest in archeology.[2] The end of the lesson is to help the student appreciate the scope, difficulty, and skills of a manipulative or physical nature as well as of an intellectual nature that archeologists must master. The beauty of this lesson is that the materials are so readily available. It demonstrates once again that inventive teachers can use most anything to help children learn.

If, then, a child indicates an interest in archeology or if you wish to create an interest, try the following.

Ask the teacher in the next room to keep a record of events in her class over the course of the day. Ask the custodian not to empty the wastebasket in that class at night.

Have your student reconstruct the day's events in the other teacher's room through careful removal and examination of the content of the wastebasket. Have the student take notes and write a report. Have your colleague check the notes and report for accuracy.

We do not wish to examine the possibilities of this lesson here in any detail, primarily because we believe that any teacher studying his wastebasket can see the many problems that will face the student archeologist. We should like to note, however, that after the report has been made, a discussion of the difficulties that face the archeologist would be appropriate. And before anyone beats us to it, let us label this the "wastebasket curriculum."

2 The lesson was developed by Charles Swenson, who was a colleague of ours when we taught at Hofstra University on Long Island.

RELATIONSHIP OF THE LESSON
TO THE STRUCTURED INDUCTIVE MODEL

We include this lesson here to point up the fact that use of a model need not be restrictive. A model is a guide, and sample or real lessons which are based upon the model need not follow it in all particulars. This lesson differs somewhat from the structured inductive model in that there is as much emphasis on techniques of investigation as there is on developing generalizations. The data which confront the child have been selected and organized by the natural events occurring in the classroom, not by the teacher.

However, the lesson is similar to the structured inductive model in that the child must use inductive thinking to arrive at a generalization, and that he is working with data which may be perceived or interpreted in various ways.

This is a good lesson to use if you want to introduce children to the reality that our knowledge of the events of the past is quite limited and probably inaccurate in many respects.

QUESTIONS TO CONSIDER
What techniques of investigation would children be using in the lesson that you planned?
Do you know what types of scholars actually use those techniques?

ASSIGNMENT V
One of the major concerns of the historian is to determine the reliability of the primary source materials which he uses. Construct a lesson which would lead fifth- or sixth-graders to discover one or more of the factors which affect the reliability of primary sources.

SAMPLE LESSON V

PROPOSITION TO BE INDUCED

Not all primary sources are reliable.

STRATEGIES TO BE EMPLOYED

Present the children with two conflicting reports by primary sources.

DATA

The following two passages which are excerpts from Commager and Nevins, *The Heritage of America.*[3]

Planters, particularly native planters, have a kind of affection for their Negroes, incredible to those who have not observed its effects. If rebellious they punish them—if well behaved, they not infrequently reward them. In health they treat them with uniform kindness, in sickness with attention and sympathy. . . . On large plantations hospitals are erected for the reception of the sick, and the best medical attendance is provided for them. The physicians of Natchez derive a large proportion of their incomes from attending plantations. On some estates a physician permanently resides, whose time may be supposed sufficiently taken up in attending to the health of from one to two hundred persons. Often several plantations, if the force on each is small, unite and employ one physician for the whole. Every plantation is supplied with suitable medicines, and generally to such an extent that some room or part of a room in the planter's house is converted into a small apothecary's shop. These, in the absence of the physician in any sudden emergency, are administered by the planter. Hence, the health of the slaves, so far as medical skill is concerned, is well provided for. They are well fed and warmly clothed in the winter, in warm jackets and trousers, and blanket coats enveloping the whole person, with hats or woolen caps and brogans. In summer they have clothing suitable to the season, and a ragged Negro is less frequently to be met with than in Northern cities. (Joseph Holt Ingraham, *The South-West by a Yankee*, 1835)

In the afternoon I made my first visit to the hospital of the estate. . . . The floor (which was not boarded, but merely the damp hard earth itself) was strewn with wretched women, who, but for their moans of pain and uneasy restless motion, might very well have each been taken for a mere heap of filthy rags. The chimney refusing passage to the smoke from the pine-wood fire, it puffed out in clouds through the room, where it circled and hung, only gradually oozing away through the windows which were so far well adapted to the purpose that there was not a single whole pane of glass in them. . . . I went on to what seemed a yet more wretched abode of wretchedness. This was a room where there was no fire because there was no chimney and where the holes made for windows had no panes or glasses in them. The shutters being closed, the place was so dark that, on first entering it, I was afraid to stir lest I should fall over some of the deplorable creatures extended upon the floor. As soon as they perceived me, one cry of "Oh, missis!" rang through the darkness, and it really seemed to me as if I was never to exhaust the pity and amazement and disgust which this receptacle of suffering humanity was to excite in me. (Frances Anne Kemble, *Journal of a Residence on a Georgian Plantation*, 1838–1839)

3 Quoted in Henry Steele Commager and Allan Nevins, *The Heritage of America* (Boston: Little, Brown and Company, 1951). Copyright 1939, 1949 by Henry Steele Commager and Allan Nevins.

PRESENTATION OF DATA

Each child will be given one of the two passages to read, and asked, "What do you learn about slavery from this report?"

In the ensuing discussion the teacher will record information on the board so that the conflicts are evident. For example:

Slaves had good medical care.   Hospitals were overcrowded and filthy.

When a good argument has developed between the two groups of children, the teacher will ask that the reports be read aloud. Then the following questions can be raised and discussed:

1. Why do these two reporters disagree?
2. Which one should we believe? Why?
3. What additional information do we need about these reporters?
4. What additional information might we need before deciding what were the "facts" about slave conditions?

When question 3 is raised, the teacher will have ready the following information about the two reporters:

Joseph Holt Ingraham—born in Maine in 1809; became a member of the faculty of Jefferson College at Washington, Mississippi; remained a Southerner the rest of his life.

Frances Anne Kemble—successful English actress; in 1834, at age twenty-five, married southern plantation owner and lived in Georgia; marriage was unsuccessful and she returned to the stage.

EVIDENCE OF CHILDREN'S LEARNING

If children can point out a variety of reasons why these reports might be unreliable, it will be assumed that they have generalized the proposition. Some expected reasons they might give are: Frances Kemble uses very "emotional" language; her unhappiness in marriage may have colored her view of the plantation; Joseph Ingraham must have favored the Southern view since he chose to live there.

Someone may point out that the two reports deal with different areas (Georgia and Mississippi), so it is hardly safe to generalize about slave conditions from this evidence, even if the two sources agreed. This will be taken as evidence that the children have learned something about testing the validity of generalizations.

At a later date, children will be presented with another passage from a primary source and asked to list the facts reported which they believe to be true and the questions they would like answered.

RELATIONSHIP OF THE LESSON
TO THE STRUCTURED INDUCTIVE MODEL

This lesson serves to point up to children the problems associated with overgeneralizing, or generalizing on the basis of too little data (in this case, one example). As in the lesson on comparative adjectives, they are faced with the necessity of evaluating the data. But in this lesson evaluation is a much more complex task.

The teacher has selected the data, and organized it to provoke disagreement among the children, because in this case it would seem that the initial disagreement will eventually lead to the desired generalization. Discussion can play an important role in the inductive process. It is through discussion that children are exposed to different viewpoints. This can serve as new data, forcing them to reexamine their own conclusions.

We might note here that the form of the "lesson plan" has varied in each of the last three lessons. We have tried to use various formats purposely to point out that form is less important than content in a lesson plan. We believe that a lesson plan which a teacher uses to teach a lesson is in essence a private communication, a message from an individual to himself. As such it should take the form that is most meaningful to that individual.

Of course a lesson plan that is prepared for use by a substitute teacher, or to explain a particular lesson to a supervisor, is another matter. In those instances the plan is a message to a second person, and the form must be one which will communicate to others.

In planning any lesson the teacher needs to clarify to himself or others the purpose of the lesson, the data or materials that will be used, the strategies or procedures to be employed, and the means by which learning will be evaluated. Any format that includes this information is a useful one.

QUESTIONS TO CONSIDER

Have you communicated each of the four major pieces of information in your lesson plan?

Was your plan prepared as a private or public communication?

ASSIGNMENT VI

The sociologist uses a variety of statistical techniques. Construct a lesson which will introduce children (at a grade level of your choice) to some elementary statistical techniques in connection with development of some aspect of the concept of "role." Some possible ideas related to role are:

a. Different family members play different roles.

b. The same person may play two different roles.

c. Some roles are related to sex.

d. Sex roles in our society are changing.

SAMPLE LESSON VI

PROPOSITION TO BE INDUCED (FOR SECOND GRADE)

Children should become aware that not all families divide jobs in the same way. At this age not all children will be able to formulate a generalization, but all should be able to see similarities and differences.

Children should also learn that counting can help us decide whether or not something is a common behavior.

STRATEGIES TO BE EMPLOYED

Children will be asked to list "things your mother does at home" and "things your father does at home." They will compare activities of their parents with those of others in the class. The number of parents engaging in each activity will be counted. Then children will be asked to divide activities into things which *most* mothers (or fathers) do and things which a *few* mothers (or fathers) do.

DATA

Children's perceptions of parental activities provide the necessary data. These perceptions also provide the teacher with additional information about the individual children in her class.

In classes where children may have only one parent, they can be asked to list activities for one *or* the other.

PRESENTATION OF THE DATA

After children have made their individual lists, they will be asked to report them while the teacher makes a composite list on the board.

When this list is complete the teacher will ask, for each of several activities in turn, "Do you think most mothers [or fathers] do this?" It is expected that there will be disagreement among the children on some activities—e.g., mowing the lawn for mothers, buying the groceries for fathers.

The teacher will then ask, "How can we decide whether this is something that most mothers or fathers do?" After some ideas have been offered, the teacher may need to ask:

"What does *most* mean?"
"What does *few* mean?"
"How many mothers do we have for this class?"
"How many of those mothers would be *most* of the mothers?"
"How many mothers would be a *few* mothers?"

When children agree on the meaning of "most" or "few" in terms of numbers for their classroom, this information should be recorded on the board. Then the teacher can ask again, "How can we tell whether most mothers in this class wash dishes [or mow the lawn]?" Some child will probably suggest counting. Children who have mothers that wash dishes can be asked to raise their hands. The number of children raising their hands will be recorded on the board next to "wash the dishes." Then the teacher will ask, "Do most of the mothers in this class wash the dishes?"

The list of activities will then be reviewed, each item in turn, and the number of mothers or fathers engaging in each activity will be recorded. Counting of hands can be done by two children at a time, giving all children a chance to count.

When all the numbers are recorded, children can be asked to make individual lists of:

Four things that most mothers do
Four things that few mothers do
Four things that most fathers do
Four things that few fathers do

EVIDENCE OF CHILDREN'S LEARNING

If children can select items to fit the above four categories, it will be assumed that they have learned that the technique of counting can help to identify common behaviors. Further evidence can be accumulated by doing a similar follow-up lesson dealing with children's activities in the home, and seeing how many know immediately that counting is a helpful procedure.

Children can be asked to go back to their original lists of parental activities and follow these directions:

"Circle the things your mother [or father] does that *most* mothers [or fathers] do."

"Put a line under the things your mother [or father] does that a *few* mothers [or fathers] do."

RELATIONSHIP OF THE LESSON
TO THE STRUCTURED INDUCTIVE MODEL

In this lesson, as in the two preceding it, children are learning a technique of investigation at the same time that they are developing generalizations. The structured inductive lesson, according to the model presented in Chapter 6, focuses particularly on teaching concepts and generalizations. But no concept can be formed without some method of investigation being used.

One of the ways in which teachers can aid children in the development of independent problem-solving skills is to teach them a variety of investigative techniques. Skills in measurement or statistical analysis, in testing reliability or accuracy of data, and in collecting data through interviews or library research are all essential to the social science investigator. And these skills are as important for the child to master as are skills in organizing data and testing and revising generalizations.

It is necessary for the teacher to plan structured inductive discovery lessons in sequences which develop children's skills in using various investigative methods, as well as in sequences that lead to greater depth of understanding of particular concepts.

QUESTIONS TO CONSIDER

If you were going to teach a follow-up lesson to the lesson you planned, what added understanding of the concept would you try to develop?

What added skills of investigation would you try to develop?

---

chapter 11

Interaction
in the Open Inductive Lesson

A chief characteristic of the open inductive discovery lesson is that it encourages greater divergency of thought. The major objective is to teach inductive methods of inquiry, particularly the process of categorizing.

Some guidelines for planning such lessons were introduced in the discussion on concept attainment. You will recall that selection and organization of data could be handled to encourage either convergent or divergent thinking. Small amounts of data, random organization of data, and open or unstructured directions for observation of data are all factors which force the student to rely more on his own resources. His problem-solving procedure becomes more a process of "assimilation," to use Piaget's term. In the everyday language of teachers we could say that the background or interest of the individual student becomes more important when less direction is provided by the teacher and the data. The result is that different students come up with different solutions to the same problem.

An actual example of this type of lesson is one in which the teacher set up a display of concrete materials, randomly organized, on a table in the front of a sixth-grade classroom. The materials were: a ball-point pen, a sheet of orange construction paper, a pair of scissors, an envelope, an artist's brush, a ruler, a sheet of stationery, a paper clip, a crayon, a sheet of graph paper, a compass (for drawing circles). Students in the class were asked to study the materials and then to make lists of things that seemed to belong together.

As students made their individual lists, the teacher walked around the room, studying them. When all the lists were nearly finished, several students were asked to place their lists on the board. The lists were as follows:

List 1 (Jane)
pen, scissors, paper clip, compass, ruler, brush
construction paper, envelope, stationery, graph paper
crayon

List 2 (Joe)
pen, brush, crayon
construction paper, envelope, stationery, graph paper
scissors, paper clip, compass, ruler

List 3 (Anne)
construction paper, crayon, brush, scissors
stationery, envelope, pen
ruler, graph paper
paper clip, compass

List 4 (Todd)
graph paper, ruler, compass
crayon, brush, pen
construction paper, stationery
paper clip, envelope
scissors

QUESTIONS TO CONSIDER
   Try to answer the following questions before you read further:
   Why did the teacher select these particular lists?
   Can you tell what criteria each child used for grouping?
   If you were the teacher in this lesson, what would your next move be?

The teacher next asked the children in the class to study Jane's list and see if they could tell why she put together the things that she did. As they suggested ideas, Jane was asked to indicate whether they were right or wrong. This same procedure was followed with each list, and in cases where the class could not explain a grouping, the maker of the list gave his reason.

The explanations were written on the board, along with the lists, in the following manner:

List 1 (Jane)

things with metal	pen, scissors, paper clip, compass, ruler, brush
all paper	construction paper, envelope, stationery, graph paper
neither group	crayon

List 2 (Joe)

mark on paper	pen, brush, crayon
paper	construction paper, envelope, stationery, graph paper
other things	scissors, paper clip, compass, ruler

List 3 (Anne)

use for art	construction paper, crayon, brush, scissors
use to write letter	stationery, envelope, pen
use to do math	ruler, graph paper
metal things	paper clip, compass

List 4 (Todd)

use for math	graph paper, ruler, compass
write on paper	crayon, brush, pen
paper	construction paper, stationery
they hold papers	paper clip, envelope
don't fit anywhere	scissors

Next the teacher asked how many children had a list exactly like Jane's list. No one did. No one had a list exactly like Joe's or Anne's or Todd's either. Several children indicated that they had one or two groups that were identical to groups on the board, however. Students were asked if they had groupings that were very different from those on the board, and these were written down for all to see.

QUESTIONS TO CONSIDER
Try to answer the following questions before you read further:
What categorizing skills do the children need to work on?
Should the teacher point out these inadequacies in this lesson?

A study of the children's reasons for grouping indicates several types of refinement that could be suggested. The most obvious is the tendency to use "miscellaneous" categories for items they cannot easily fit into their major categories. This is a common problem, and one that the teacher should expect from children who are just beginning to develop their skills in categorizing.

Another general problem (if these four lists are typical) would seem to be that the categories are not all discrete, yet the children have done no "cross-categorizing." For example, Anne's category of *metal things* should include scissors, which she has placed under *use for art*. Scissors really belong in both categories, because they are overlapping categories. In Todd's list, the graph paper should be included under *paper* as well as under *use for math*. Faced with this problem, the teacher might choose to work on ways to refine categories so that they are discrete, that is, so that each item belongs in one and only one category. At this stage, however, it may be better to develop children's awareness of the "problem" by getting them to cross-categorize. (Their mathematics work may be usefully applied here. They might draw Venn diagrams on the board, or use yarn loops to enclose objects on a table, showing that some objects belong within two circles.)

In this lesson the teacher did not point out these problems to the children. She merely asked how many children had groups which were composed of things that didn't fit anywhere else. More than half the class did. She also asked if anyone had an item listed in more than one group. Only two children had done this.

The teacher was using this lesson to learn more about the children's abilities, rather than to instruct them. Later she would plan lessons to improve their skills in the needed areas.

The next question the teacher asked in this lesson was: Which of these lists is right? A lengthy discussion ensued as students defended one list against another. Finally one girl suggested that they were all right, because everyone had different ideas about what went together. The class heartily approved this idea, and the lesson ended on that note.

INTERACTION TECHNIQUES

It was suggested earlier that selecting and organizing data for an open inductive discovery lesson is not a difficult process. In this case familiar materials which lent themselves to a variety of interpretations were randomly organized, and an open question was asked. These techniques were aimed at encouraging divergent thinking. And it is evident from the variety of lists produced that the techniques were successful.

It is imperative that appropriate interactive techniques be used in an open inductive lesson, however, for divergent thinking can too easily be cut off. The important techniques used by the teacher in this lesson were:

1. She allowed sufficient time for students to complete their lists individually before comparisons were made.
2. She selected lists for public display that illustrated a wide variety of bases for grouping.
3. She initially had children explain or analyze each other's lists, thereby focusing attention on *understanding* rather than *evaluating* the ideas generated.
4. She encouraged student-to-student interaction by having Jane, Joe, Anne, and Todd indicate whether the children's explanations of their reasoning were correct. This provided the feeling that a variety of "authorities" existed, each student being an authority on his own thinking.

5. She rewarded divergent productions by writing additional groupings that were "different" on the board.
6. She refrained from pointing out the inadequacies of the lists in this lesson.
7. She asked children which list was "right" only after it was clear to the class that each list was reasonable and that a large variety of lists existed. She accepted and supported the idea that all the lists were right.

ACCEPTING VS. APPROVING STUDENT IDEAS

There is a fine line between teacher acceptance and teacher approval of student ideas which becomes crucial to effective interaction in an open inductive discovery lesson. Teacher approval implies that an idea is correct, and tends to stop the flow of alternative ideas. Examples of comments which could be called teacher approval of an idea are: "Yes"; "That's right"; "Exactly"; "Very good"; and "Of course."

Teacher acceptance, on the other hand, suggests that the idea is worthy of consideration by the group. It is the group, not the teacher, who will eventually decide whether or not it is correct. In the meantime, other alternative ideas are also worthy of consideration. Examples of responses which could be called teacher acceptance are: "Okay"; "That's an interesting idea"; "I hadn't thought of that"; and writing the idea down on the blackboard for other students to see.

It is important that students be encouraged, even coaxed along, when they are attempting to use divergent thinking skills. For years divergent ideas have been locked out of classrooms by teachers who have ridiculed them or admonished children to "stick to the point." The years have taken their toll. Children do not like to be made fun of. Most will be hesitant about offering divergent ideas until they are assured that there is some advantage to doing so. That is why teacher acceptance becomes so crucial.

There are other ways in which the teacher can provide acceptance and support for divergent ideas. One technique is the use of paraphrasing. In this instance the teacher restates the student's idea in slightly different words, and asks, "Is that what you mean?" or "Is that what you're saying?" (E.g., "You're suggesting, Todd, that we put papers inside an envelope, and we also put them 'inside' a paper clip, is that it?") This serves to clarify the idea in everyone's mind, brings it to the attention of the whole group, and in effect is a more extensive way of accepting student ideas.

Another alternative is to compare the idea with one which has already been presented. (E.g., "Let's see, Anne. Your group of *metal things* includes things that are made entirely of metal. That's a bit different from Jane's group of things that have *some metal* in them.") This comparison implies no value judgment—only that the two ideas have some similarity and some difference. This technique has the virtue of bringing two ideas to the attention of the group at the same time. In effect, the teacher is accepting one idea, and "reaccepting" a previous idea— that is, providing additional rewards and encouragement.

POSTPONING EVALUATION

Paraphrasing and comparing student ideas are techniques which also focus attention on understanding the ideas. This has the desirable effect of postponing evaluation of the ideas till a later time.

Obviously, evaluation of generalizations is a necessary part of the inductive process and a skill that children need to develop. Premature evaluation, however, tends to slow down or even end the production of alternative ideas. Children may in effect say to themselves, "If you're just going to criticize everyone's ideas, why *should* I bother to give one." In an open inductive discovery lesson it is important, therefore, that the teacher avoid making evaluative comments himself, and also that he discourage or forestall evaluative comments by other children. It is not advisable in *this* type of lesson for the teacher to say, "What do the rest of you think of that idea? Do you agree?"

Successful problem solving results from the ability to use two very different, perhaps even incompatible, styles of thinking *at the appropriate times.* The first style involves generating possible alternative solutions to a problem, hypothesizing if you will, and it is a form of thinking that requires free-floating associations of data, open exploration, and the suspension of judgment. The second style involves testing alternative solutions to a problem, systematically evaluating their effectiveness in responding to the conditions that exist. It is a form of thinking that requires application of critical judgments and the ability to operate comfortably in closed systems. If the second style of thinking is applied too soon, not very many solutions will be generated and effective solutions may never be produced. If evaluative thinking is never applied, the problem may never be solved for another reason. Trial-and-error applications of possible solutions to a problem lead not only to repeated failure, but also to eventual frustration, and probable retreat from the problem.

The teacher who wants to develop problem-solving abilities needs to help children learn to *separate* the two styles of thinking, as well as to use both effectively. In the open inductive discovery lesson, the focus is on the production of ideas. Evaluation of ideas must be temporarily postponed. Note that in the lesson discussed above, when the teacher did move to a form of evaluation, it was presented in a positive way. She asked which list was right. This structured children's comments to defend particular ideas, or to say what was *good* about the lists, rather than to criticize or note what was bad about them.

But even this mild and supportive form of evaluation was postponed until an effort had been made to analyze and understand the ideas presented. The teacher defined the student role early in the lesson by asking children to try to figure out why Jane had grouped the items as she did. This turned the group's attention away from evaluation and indicated the teacher's belief that Jane's idea was a reasonable one, worthy of other's consideration.

REWARDING PRODUCTION OF IDEAS

All of the forms of attention mentioned above are means of rewarding children for their production of ideas. Social recognition is a very effective reward, particularly when it comes from both peers and teachers. Intrinsic rewards also exist, of course. For most children it is fun to play with various types of data and to generate new ideas.

One other effective type of social recognition is using the inventor's name to identify the invention.[1] The world talks about Whitney's cotton gin and Einstein's theory of relativity. Why not Judy's Classification System or Arnold's Rule for Capitalization? This particular technique is as effective in semideductive or structured inductive lessons as it is in the open inductive lesson. An elementary class might discuss, evaluate, and refine Andy's Property of Addition for several weeks before being told that mathematicians call the same phenomenon the "commutative property." Their understanding of the property will not be any less, and Andy will have gained a great deal of recognition for his discovery.

FOLLOW-UP LESSONS

We have suggested that the open inductive lesson functions most effectively as an introductory lesson. It provides children with an oppor-

---

[1] This technique was first explicated to us in detail by Paul Niquette, of the Xerox Corporation's Education Division, and Joan McCrory, a student teacher at the California State College at Hayward. Both are very adept in use of discovery methods.

tunity to practice skills in categorizing and divergent thinking. It provides the teacher with information on needed refinements of children's categorizing skills. Follow-up lessons will be necessary to develop these refined skills, and to introduce some of the criteria that can be used to evaluate category systems.

The two problem areas noted in the illustrative lesson were use of miscellaneous or catchall categories and use of nondiscrete categories. Some techniques that can be used to refine children's categorizing skills in relation to these problems are exercises in "stretching" categories, in forming single-element categories, and in delineating the functions of categories.

STRETCHING CATEGORIES

One of the characteristics of the divergent thinker is that he tends to use "wide category bands."[2] That is, he tends to extend the limits of a category in order to admit items that don't quite fit. In this way he makes less use of catchall categories, because he has fewer items that don't fit his main categories. Children can learn to extend or stretch their categories in order to admit additional items.

An example of an exercise which helps to develop this skill is one dealing with classification of animals. A number of large pictures of various animals are set up around the room. Children are asked to form two groups of animals, using these pictures. They need *not* include all of the pictures in their groups. One child is called on to select and organize pictures to illustrate the two groups he has formed. (If the pictures are carefully selected, the variety of possibilities is quite large—e.g., meat-eaters and plant-eaters; large animals and small animals; flying animals and swimming animals; zoo animals and wild animals, etc.)

The class must study the pictures selected to determine what categories are being illustrated. Once the categories have been confirmed, the teacher selects a picture which was not included as illustrative of either category and asks the class in which category this picture belongs.

The idea is to select a picture which does not easily fit into either category. The picture may come from the original group provided to the children, or from a group of alternative pictures that the teacher has kept in reserve. The children must now change or extend one of the categories to accommodate the new example. Some possible picture selections and category extensions are indicated in Table 11–1. Practice such as this in stretching categories can later be applied to revising the

---

[2] M. A. Wallach and N. Kogan, *Modes of Thinking in Young Children* (New York: Holt, Rinehart and Winston, 1965).

TABLE 11-1

Original Categories	Selected Picture	Category Extension
Meat-eaters and plant-eaters	An omnivorous animal, such as man or an ant at a picnic	Either category can be extended to include animals who eat both plant products and meat products
Meat-eaters and plant-eaters	A mouse, eating cheese; a cat, drinking milk; or a weasel, eating eggs	Extend the meat-eaters to include eaters of "dairy" products
Large animals (e.g., elephant, giraffe) and small animals (e.g., fly, spider)	A medium-sized animal, such as a lizard, turtle, sheep, dog	Extend either category to include animals of moderate size; or extend "large" category to include moderately large (sheep, dog) and "small" category to include moderately small (lizard, turtle)
Flying animals and swimming animals	A duck or goose	Extend either category to include animals which do both
Flying animals and swimming animals	A squirrel or rabbit	Extend either category to include animals which do neither
Zoo animals and wild animals	A cat, dog, or canary	Extend zoo category to include pets
Zoo animals (including pets) and wild animals	A cow, horse, or pig	Extend zoo category to include domesticated animals

categories that children have formed previously in the introductory open inductive lesson. The teacher can form a group of children who used catchall categories and together they can work to extend the other categories they used to include these miscellaneous items.

Stretching exercises also develop skills necessary in revising generalizations on the basis of new, contradictory data. This is a crucial skill to develop if inductive discovery methods are to be used over a long-term period.

FORMING SINGLE-ELEMENT CATEGORIES

Another skill which can help to eliminate catchall categories is the ability to form a set or category containing only one element. Piaget's studies have indicated children's general unwillingness to do this.[3] Many adults are also unwilling. You, yourself, while doing the exercises in Chapter 2, may have resisted forming a category of one item (such as the rattle) when you were asked to form groups from the list of words presented.

An exercise which can help children to develop this skill would be to provide them with examples of members of categories, one containing several elements, and the other containing only one element. The teacher can define the category containing several elements, and have the children indicate what the possibilities for the single-element category might be.

For example, children could be shown a group on a felt board containing two small squares (red and blue), two small circles (blue and yellow), and two small triangles (yellow and red). The teacher would identify this as a group of small geometric figures. Next she would show them a single large red circle, and ask what group or category this belonged to.

The children might immediately identify this as belonging to a group of *large* geometric figures. In this event, the teacher would shift to a new group of several elements for comparison with the red circle. The new group might be two small squares (red and blue), two large squares (blue and yellow), and two "giant" squares (yellow and red). The teacher would identify this as a group of squares, and ask what group the large red circle might belong to now, the expected answer being "circles."

In the event that the children provide other answers to the first problem, such as "red figures" or "circles," the teacher can say: "If this [the red circle] represents a group of red geometric figures, some members of our first group of small geometric figures would also belong in the second group. Which items would they be?"

[3] Barbel Inhelder and Jean Piaget, *The Early Growth of Logic in the Child* (New York: Harper and Row, 1964).

The children will probably see that the small red square and the small red triangle belong in both groups. And the teacher might then ask, "Can anyone think of a group for the red circle that would *not* include any of the members of the group of small geometric figures?" At this point children will probably see that the large red circle can belong to a group of large geometric figures, and that that differentiates it from the group of small geometric figures with which they have been comparing it.

In this type of exercise the children are being introduced to the possibilities of single-element categories (categories or groups containing only one item). At the same time, they are beginning to learn the difference between discrete and nondiscrete categories, although these terms are not being used. (Discrete categories, you will recall, are those in which each item can fit in one and only one category.)

A variation on this exercise would be to spread out an assortment of objects on a table—e.g., a ball, a banana, an orange crayon, a marshmallow, a rough stone, a leaf, etc. The teacher would hold up one object—in this case an orange. She would say: "This orange belongs to a group or category of things. Can you think of a group it might belong to?" Children will probably think of some categories without prompting, for example, "fruit." The teacher can write these on the board, and ask which of the items on the table would also belong to this group. When children run out of possible categories, the teacher can hold up, next to the orange, an item from the table, and ask how these two things are alike. As the similarities are identified, they can be listed on the board as additional category possibilities. For the assortment of objects listed above, the categories generated could be: round things, fruit, orange-colored things, things to eat, rough-textured things, and things that grow on trees.

These two exercises serve to demonstrate to children that: (1) a single item can be representative of a wide variety of groups or categories; (2) one way of defining a *particular* category that the single item can represent is to select another item (available or imagined) with which to compare it; and (3) another way of defining a particular category for the single item to represent is to contrast the item with other categories you have already formed.

Once the children have learned this last procedure well, the exercise suggested earlier for stretching categories can be varied to provide additional practice in this skill. In this variation, after the two groups of animals have been identified, a nontypical picture is selected, and the teacher asks, "What *new* group can we add that would include this animal?" If the two groups are meat-eaters and plant-eaters, and the nontypical example is a man, the new category might be animals that eat both meat and plants, or possibly animals that eat prepared (cooked, etc.) foods.

DELINEATING CATEGORY FUNCTIONS

Additional skill in the formation of discrete categories can be developed through exercises which emphasize the functions which category systems might serve. This is another step in introducing criteria by which children can evaluate their category systems.

As a follow-up to the open inductive lesson described at the beginning of this chapter, the teacher might divide the class into groups and provide each group with a different function for the categorizing of the various items. One group could organize the items for the purpose of displaying them for sale in a stationery store. Another group could organize them for use by children in a classroom. A third group could organize them for use by a secretary in a business office. (This latter group might include a category of "things not used in the office.")

Comparison of the category systems produced by the three groups could point up the fact that different functions or purposes lead to different category systems. An important question to ask in understanding future groupings of classmates may then be, "What can it be used for?"

The fact that they are being asked to form groupings which will determine an item's placement in space (location in a stationery store, classroom, or office) will open up to children the problem of nondiscrete categories. Obviously the same item cannot be placed simultaneously in two different locations in space. They now have a reason for trying to produce discrete categories.

APPLICATION OF IMPROVED CATEGORIZING SKILLS

The follow-up lessons suggested here all grow out of common "inadequacies" in the categorizing skills of both children and adults. They are lessons which involve somewhat more structuring or direction than the open inductive lesson, but they share its major objective of teaching inductive methods of inquiry.

The skills in divergent and evaluative thinking developed through these lessons can be put to good use in lessons of the semideductive and structured inductive type. The open inductive lesson and the suggested follow-up lessons produce concepts related to process rather than content. But in the long run they contribute to the efficiency and effectiveness of children's formation of concepts related to content. For this reason they are an important type of discovery lesson and should not be neglected.

ASSIGNMENT

As we have tried to point out in this chapter, classroom interaction is very important to the success of an open inductive discovery lesson. Therefore, we suggest that a valuable activity for you will be to tape-record yourself teaching an open inductive lesson. When you play back the tape, listen for your reactions to children's comments. How many times do you use each of the following types of reaction?

Reactions to
be Avoided
{
Approval
Disapproval
Asking other students to evaluate the idea
}

Reactions to
be Encouraged
{
Acceptance (verbal)
Recording idea on chalkboard
Paraphrasing idea
Comparing to another idea
Referring to an idea by the name of the "inventor"
Asking student for further explanation of the idea
}

Before you play back your taped lesson to evaluate your classroom inter-action, you may want to reread the section on interaction techniques.

---

chapter **12**

Sample Lessons
of the Open Inductive Type

We have been discussing the importance of developing skill in using interaction patterns that are appropriate to the open inductive lesson. But the planning of open inductive lessons is also an important skill.

Remember that small amounts of data, random organization of data, and open or unstructured directions for observation of data will help to encourage divergent thinking. Keeping this in mind, plan an open inductive lesson for children at a grade level of your choice. The open inductive lesson does not focus on subject matter content, but you may find it helpful to select materials or general topics from language arts, social studies, or science to get you started.

In this chapter we suggest four possible topics for lessons, and present plans for lessons developed around these topics. You may select any one of the four suggested assignments, or develop one of your own. Once again we urge that you plan a lesson of your own *before* reading the sample lessons we have provided. As was the case in previous chapters, the sample lessons presented here have all been taught successfully to children.

ASSIGNMENT I

   Construct an open inductive discovery lesson dealing with the general topic of mass media of communication.

SAMPLE LESSON I

MATERIALS TO BE USED

Television programs will be the materials to be categorized.

PROCEDURES TO BE USED

Children will be asked to name all the television programs they can think of. As they name them, the programs will be listed on the board.

When a fairly lengthy list has been developed (fifteen to twenty programs), children will be asked to organize the programs into groups. Each child will work alone, forming his groups and writing them down. Children can add more programs to their own lists if they wish.

Several children will be asked to report on the groupings that they used. The bases or criteria used for grouping will be compared and discussed.

POSSIBLE RESULTS

The kinds of groups formed could vary greatly. Some possible bases for grouping are: programs I watch, programs I don't watch; daytime programs, nighttime programs; programs on ABC, programs on NBC, programs on CBS, programs on the Educational Television Network; cartoons, comedy, mystery, animal shows, news, etc.

SUGGESTED FOLLOW-UP LESSON

Children could be divided into several small groups. A copy of *TV Guide* could be provided to each group. The children could be asked to study the *TV Guide* to determine what kinds of categories or groupings were used in organizing it (e.g., time and channel). They could compare this organization with their own organizations and discuss alternative purposes or functions of their groupings.

As another possibility, children could be provided with lists of programs based on Nielsen ratings. They could discuss the purpose of this kind of categorizing of programs and discuss its effects on their own viewing habits.

RELATIONSHIP OF THE LESSON
TO THE OPEN INDUCTIVE MODEL

In this lesson children are encouraged to use divergent, inductive thinking. The main factors affecting thinking are the unstructured directions or questions and the random organization of data. The materials are familiar to the children because they are provided by the children. Because they are materials not generally used in school, the meanings which children attach to them are apt to be highly individual. All of these things encourage a variety of responses from the children.

No particular concept is aimed at in this lesson, but children are gaining skill in organizing data. This is the major purpose of any open inductive discovery lesson.

QUESTION TO CONSIDER
What techniques did you use to encourage divergent thinking in your lesson?

ASSIGNMENT II
Construct an open inductive discovery lesson dealing with the general topic of ecology.

SAMPLE LESSON II

MATERIALS TO BE USED

Debris and rubbish collected from the school playground or an adjacent neighborhood.

PROCEDURES TO BE USED

Children will be taken on a walk to collect debris and rubbish. (This may be collected in their yards and neighborhoods the night before, if this seems desirable.)

Upon their return to the classroom, children will be asked to place their collections on their desks and to group the items they have collected, putting together the things they think belong together.

Small groups can be formed of children who sit near each other. These groups can share their organizations of materials with each other, explaining why they put particular items together.

Another possible procedure is to spread sheets of construction paper on the floor in a large circle and have children group their collections on these. Then the explanations of groupings can be shared with the whole class, and they can all see the materials being discussed.

POSSIBLE RESULTS

In this exercise children will each have different items to group, so a wide variety of results is quite probable. Some of the kinds of bases for groupings which might be used are: type of material (metal, paper, wood); shape of material (long, round, square, etc.); condition of material (torn, dirty, crumpled, clean, etc.); source of material (people dropped it, wind blew it).

SUGGESTED FOLLOW-UP LESSONS

Children could be paired and asked to add the items from one child's collection to the groups formed by the other child. They could then discuss whether they had to make any changes in the groups when new items were added.

Children might visit a local ecological collection center to see how materials collected there are categorized and stored. They might then visit the local rubbish dump and see whether any categorizing of materials occurs there. The differences in purposes and categorizing procedures of these two establishments could be discussed.

The children could make collages of the materials they have collected. The differences between organizing materials to put similar items together and organizing them to create interesting designs could be discussed.

RELATIONSHIP OF THE LESSON
TO THE OPEN INDUCTIVE MODEL

In this lesson the factors which encourage divergent, inductive thinking are: the small amount of data available to each child (unless they searched in a particularly dirty area); the fact that each child had different data; the random organization of data (the only organization other than the child's would be the order in which items were found); the unstructured directions for grouping data.

The suggested follow-up lesson where pairs of children combine their data could lead to experiences in "category stretching." An item which did not quite fit an established category might cause the children to redefine the category to include the new item.

The other suggested follow-up lessons deal with the different functions of category systems or organizations of materials. Children can begin to see that for some purposes little or no organization of materials is necessary—e.g., dumping rubbish. They can also see that for some purposes it is better to combine objects which are dissimilar—e.g., artistic arrangements.

QUESTIONS TO CONSIDER

In your lesson, did you identify follow-up activities which would develop children's skills in categorizing, such as exercises in "stretching" categories, in forming single-element categories, or in identifying the functions of various category systems?

If not, can you think of some activities of that type now?

ASSIGNMENT III

Construct an open inductive discovery lesson dealing with the general topic of invention.

SAMPLE LESSON III[1]

MATERIALS TO BE USED

A bowl, a pot, and a spoon. These can be made of metal, wood, ceramics, or any other common material. They do not need to be made of the same material. The pot should be one with a long handle, as a saucepan or frying pan has.

PROCEDURE TO BE FOLLOWED

Ask children to agree on names for the objects. Have them study the objects quietly for a minute. Ask:

"How are these objects alike?"
"How are they different?"
"Did people always have objects like these?"
"Did these objects appear all at once?"
"If not, which came first?"

Let children discuss each question in turn. Accept all responses or suggestions.

If children raise questions, open them up to other children in the group and/or write them down on the board to be answered later. Avoid answering them yourself, even if you know the answer.

POSSIBLE RESULTS

When this lesson was taught to a group of six "slow" fifth-graders, the following ideas were a few of the many produced:

[1] This lesson was planned by Joan McCrory, a student teacher at California State College at Hayward, and was taught to fifth-grade children.

1. Bowls came before pots; a pot is a bowl with a handle attached. Spoons may be miniature pots, or they could originally have been sticks (handles) that someone attached a small bowl to.
2. Man-made objects often copy things found in nature—e.g., handles copy sticks, bowls copy shells.
3. Inventions are partly accidental. But if you don't *need* something, you might not notice the accident. So needing things results in inventing them.
4. Thinking is more fun than having teachers tell you what you should learn.
5. Put two everyday objects together and ask "which came first" and you will probably learn something you didn't know you knew.
6. A good way to investigate something is to check what you already know, then look up the part that you know you *don't* know. This saves time.
7. We agree a bird's nest is not an invention, but houses are. Why?
8. *Homo sapiens* is not a good name. We are really *"Homo inventor."* People don't just go around thinking and knowing things. They *make* things.
9. If making things is inventing, is a story an invention? Are art things inventions?
10. Because I am human, I may invent something, someday.

SUGGESTED FOLLOW-UP LESSONS

The types of follow-up here will depend largely on the ideas and questions raised by the children. Follow-up investigations should probably be determined by the group or by individual students in the group. Some possibilities are: checking other people's definitions of "invention"; looking for early examples of bowls, pots, and spoons in various cultures (available in museums or picture books); take three more common objects and see what new ideas are produced; try to combine two objects to make an invention of your own; read about inventions which resulted from accidents (Charles Lamb's essay on the origin of roast pig or the discovery of penicillin).

RELATIONSHIP OF THE LESSON TO THE OPEN INDUCTIVE MODEL

This lesson uses both divergent inductive and divergent deductive thinking. Divergent thought is encouraged by the use of a very small amount of data and of open questions which invite children to observe the data in new ways.

The focus in this lesson is upon techniques of investigation, but in this case the technique is not limited to categorizing. Children are asked to observe, to compare, and to hypothesize about possible relationships among the data. The group of children with whom this lesson was tried moved very quickly into the problems which any investigator confronts, such as definition of terms.

One of the interesting results of this lesson was the number of questions raised by the children themselves. In order to keep divergent thought flowing, it was very important that the teacher refrain from providing answers to these questions.

Sometimes teachers feel that children's curiosity should not be unsatisfied. But a crucial part of being an effective investigator is being able to maintain your curiosity long enough to hunt for an answer to your own question. Children can only develop this ability if teachers allow them to go on wondering about some things.

QUESTIONS TO CONSIDER

In the lesson you planned, would children be expected to use both inductive and deductive thinking?

What questions would you expect the *children* to generate in your lesson?

How many ways could these questions be answered *without* the teacher providing the answer?

ASSIGNMENT IV

Construct an open inductive lesson dealing with the general topic of geography.

SAMPLE LESSON IV[2]

MATERIALS TO BE USED

A large felt board, and felt cutouts representing: a bay, a lake, hills, trees, parks, railroad tracks, large houses, small houses, apartment houses, factories, and schools. (The elements provided can and should be varied to suit the *local* topography and economic structure.) Large pieces of white drawing paper.

---

2 This lesson was developed by Janet Vierra, a student teacher at California State College at Hayward, and was taught successfully to fifth-grade students.

PROCEDURE TO BE USED

Tell the children that they are going to design a community. They will all have the same elements (list these on the board or on a handout to be distributed) but they can arrange these any way they like. Most of the children will draw their communities on paper and write brief explanations of why they placed things where they did. A small group of children will work on the felt board, deciding together how their community will look.

When the designs are completed they can be set up around the room, giving children ample opportunity to study each other's productions. The felt-board community will then be discussed by the group as a whole. Children can suggest changes in the spacial arrangements and indicate why they think certain elements belong near each other or apart from each other.

POSSIBLE RESULTS

When this lesson was carried out with fifth-grade children in a prosperous suburban community, the following relationships were discussed:

1. The schools should be near the houses because the kids have to walk to school.
2. The factories should be near the railroad tracks so they can get their supplies and send out the things they make.
3. The factories should be in the hills away from town so they don't pollute the air where everyone lives.
4. The factories should be near where the people live so the people can get to work without much driving. Cars pollute the air too.
5. The parks should be near the apartment houses so the kids without yards have someplace to play.
6. The parks should be in the hills near the big houses. The people with big houses are the ones who pay the taxes to build the parks, so they should get to use them.
7. The big houses should be together, and the small houses should be together, and the apartment houses should be together because people who are the same should live together.
8. The apartment houses should be near the factories and the big houses should be far away from the factories, because the factory workers probably live in the apartment houses.
9. The men who run the factories probably live in the big houses, so they ought to have their houses near where they work too.

SUGGESTED FOLLOW-UP LESSONS

Children could take a tour of several near-by communities to see whether the patterns they have suggested exist in the communities in their area. They could study maps of communities in other parts of the country and in other cultures of the world to see what different kinds of arrangements exist. They might meet with city planners or officials who administer building codes in their area to learn what restrictions govern possible arrangements of buildings in their community.

RELATIONSHIP OF THE LESSON
TO THE OPEN INDUCTIVE MODEL

In this lesson children are using established categories to examine possible relationships among different categories. In most instances they will form generalizations or relationships on the basis of past experience and observation. The more heterogeneous the class, the more these observations will vary.

The factors which contribute to divergent thinking in this lesson are the random organization of the data or elements given to the children and the unstructured directions. Another important factor in this lesson will be time. The children will need plenty of time to try out ideas for different arrangements. (Some of them will need plenty of paper as well.) This lesson will probably take several days to complete.

The felt board and movable elements contribute to the effectiveness of the discussion by making it possible to try out ideas about different arrangements. It would probably be a great advantage if children could design their individual maps using paper cutouts or blocks instead of simply drawing symbols on a paper. They would then be freer to move things around in various relationships.

This lesson deals with a technique of investigation which is used particularly by the geographer, the anthropologist, and the sociologist. All of these social scientists are skilled in observing man's uses of space. In this lesson children are not told what spacial patterns exist, but the activity of forming patterns of their own serves to sharpen their observation of the world around them.

This lesson is also rather unique in that it raises questions of value. We suggest that it is useful for children to investigate their own values and compare them to those of others around them, just as it is useful for them to compare their more objective perceptions. In discussions of values, as in discussions of other divergent viewpoints, it is good strategy for the teacher to remain neutral, permitting students to put forth their own ideas in an accepting climate. In some instances it will be important for the teacher to clarify *facts* which are in question, but premature expressions of his opinions or values will probably keep the children from seriously considering their own values.

QUESTION TO CONSIDER

Does the lesson you planned give children practice in the use of a technique of investigation generally used by people who study the particular topic you chose?

chapter 13

Artistic Perception and the Transductive Discovery Lesson

Transductive thinking involves comparing or relating two items which are seen to have some similarities. One example of transductive thinking is the use of analogy. Transductive thinking tends to yield results which are divergent. It is the type of thinking typically used by creative artists, such as poets, painters, and composers.

Probably the most common and obvious example of transductive thinking in the world of the elementary school child is the television commercial. There may be those who would dispute the fact that people who create commercials are using artistic thinking, but there is a basic similarity between the process of relating qualities of a cat to qualities of fog, as Carl Sandburg did, and the process of relating qualities of a cigarette to qualities of springtime, as one familiar commercial did.

Because transductive thinking tends to be highly divergent thinking, children will need assurance that the risk-taking this involves is valued by the teacher. One way to do this is to introduce the transductive discovery process with a lesson which shows its legitimate uses in society. The following lesson is an example.

SAMPLE LESSON I

PROPOSITIONS TO BE INDUCED

"Scientific" observations are different from "artistic" observations. Both kinds of observations are valuable.

STRATEGIES TO BE EMPLOYED

Give children two lists which contain pairs of items which are similar in some way. Have them determine how the two lists differ.

DATA

The lists will be as follows:

man—mouse	cat—fog
man—monkey	car—cougar
ice—water	snow—blanket
tornado—hurricane	tornado—scouring powder
iron—aluminum	steel—muscle
salt—sugar	bread—money
pine—oak	autumn—old age

PRESENTATION OF DATA

Children will be told that somebody thought each pair of items were alike in some way and their job is to find out how the two lists differ.

The teacher will ask for each pair of items in the left-hand list:

"How are these items alike?"
"Who might put these items together, or say they are similar?"

Children's responses to these questions will be recorded on the board, e.g.:

Pair of Items	How Alike?	Who Says So?
man—mouse	Both are alive; we test diseases of man on mice	Biologist, doctor, or medical researcher
ice—water	Both forms of water	Scientist
tornado—hurricane	Both strong winds; both cause damage; not too common	Weatherman

The same procedure will be followed with the right-hand list. Children will probably be able to identify similarities but may have trouble deciding "who says so?" The teacher should have some poems and advertisements ready for use in this case—e.g., Carl Sandburg's *Fog*.

Next the teacher will ask children to suggest pairs of items, and he will record them in the appropriate list. After a while the child giving the pair of items can indicate what list they belong in and other children asked whether or not they agree on this placement.

Finally the teacher can ask for a summary statement as to how the two lists differ. She will also ask which list is a "better" example of pairs of similar items. Children will probably disagree on their responses here, and follow-up questions can be asked, such as:

"How can we use these comparisons?"
"Is that an important use?"
"Is one kind of use more important than another?"

At some point in the lesson the teacher may want to ask children to try adding a third item to each of the pairs, one which fits in with both members of the pair. It is expected that they will find it easier to think of additional items for the pairs in the left-hand list than for the pairs in the right-hand list.

EVIDENCE OF CHILDREN'S LEARNING

Children's ability to add items to the two lists and to verbalize differences between the two lists will indicate how much understanding they have.

At some later time children might be asked to make both scientific and artistic comparisons for a single item, e.g., an interestingly shaped piece of driftwood. If they can make "scientific" comparisons based on similarities of structure, function, or composition and make "artistic" comparisons which show divergent or imaginative thinking, this will be accepted as evidence that they have grasped the desired concept.

FORMS OF COMPOSITION

Once children are convinced that such divergent thinking is valuable the transductive discovery lesson can be used to good advantage in developing the skills of inquiry used by artists in various fields. Most of these skills relate to the process of composition.

Creative writing is the form of composition most familiar to elementary school children and their teachers. Exercises in use of transductive thinking can contribute substantially to development and refinement of creative writing skills. One of the best sets of materials we know of for this purpose is the *Making It Strange* series of booklets, prepared by Synectics, Inc., and published by Harper and Row.

In these booklets children work on exercises like the following:

How is a cloud like a whisper? Name all the ways you can think of.
Which is louder, a smile or a frown? Tell why you think so.
You are a refrigerator. How do you look? What do you have inside you?
     How do you feel?

Musical and visual forms of composition are less familiar to both teachers and children. We would not expect that elementary school children would become skilled composers in either field, but they can begin to explore some of the concepts which guide the mature artist. Two of these concepts are *form* and *pattern*.

The sample lessons that follow are presented as illustrations of the kinds of lessons that can be developed to encourage children's transductive discovery in art and music through use of these concepts.

SAMPLE LESSON II

OBJECTIVES

To identify common visual forms. To explore various arrangements of forms, producing different patterns.

DATA

Familiar data will be most useful here. Children will be led to view this familiar data from a new perspective.

It is suggested that data be supplied or identified by the children. One means for collection of data is to provide a group of children with one or more Polaroid cameras, and take them for a walk in the neighborhood. Each child will take one or more photographs of something that looks interesting to him.

If no cameras are available, children can be asked to recall something that they saw on their walk, and work from memory rather than from an actual photograph.

PROCEDURES

Have children identify the shapes that are present in their photograph (or in the picture in their mind). Most children will probably see geometric shapes quite readily. Others may see other forms, such as an S or an A, in their pictures.

Let children cut out shapes similar to those in their photograph, using colored construction paper. Their shapes will be on a larger scale than those in the photograph. They might begin work with these shapes by reconstructing their photograph as an abstract arrangement. This will focus their attention on the forms that exist in their picture (reality) and on the spatial relationships between and among the forms.

Next children can be asked to take the same construction-paper shapes or forms, and to experiment with various rearrangements of them. When they find an arrangement that is pleasing to them, they can make it permanent by gluing or pasting it on a large sheet of paper.

Later discussion of their compositions can deal with elements of patterns that they have produced. For example: Do their patterns involve repetition of forms? Is there variation of form (the same form in different sizes, or different forms)? How do their rearranged patterns differ from the original patterns that existed in reality?

EVALUATION

Do children demonstrate more awareness of form and pattern in later visual compositions?

RELATIONSHIP OF THE LESSON TO THE TRANSDUCTIVE MODEL

In this lesson children are relating abstract forms to the visual reality around them. They can then proceed to use this relationship to experiment with the production of different visual patterns. The use of construction-paper shapes makes such experimentation simpler for children in the concrete stage of development.

The children are utilizing a technique of investigation commonly used by the visual artist, which is to rearrange or emphasize certain forms or elements existing in reality, in order to produce a more personal interpretation of that reality.

SAMPLE LESSON III

OBJECTIVES

To differentiate between melodic patterns and nonmelodic patterns.
To explore simple musical forms.

DATA

Asking children to produce melodies out of thin air would probably be very difficult for some. One source of data which is readily available and which has some personal meaning for the child is his telephone number.[1] A telephone number consists of a sequence of numbers that

---

[1] This procedure was brought to our attention by Janine Brobst, an elementary music teacher in Bradford Woods, Pennsylvania.

can easily be transformed into notes on the scale—say, with $0 = $ ti, $1 = $ do, $2 = $ re, $3 = $ mi, $4 = $ fa, $5 = $ sol, $6 = $ la, $7 = $ ti, $8 = $ do, and $9 = $ re. The telephone number 273-5642 thus produces the tone pattern, re, ti, mi, sol, la, fa, re. Some telephone numbers will produce tone patterns that are pleasing and easy to sing, and others will not.

PROCEDURES

Elementary school children probably do not know enough about music notation to write down melodies in standard notational form. Each child can be given a diagram of a piano keyboard, with middle C as do, as shown in Fig. 13–1.

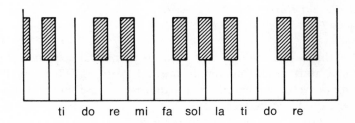

ti   do   re   mi   fa   sol   la   ti   do   re

Fig. 13–1

He can write his own telephone number below the keyboard, and then write the translation of that number in musical syllables. He can practice "playing" his sequence of notes on the diagram, and when he is fairly adept, he can play it on a real piano and listen to the tone pattern it produces.

If there is no piano in the classroom, a trip to a room that does have a piano can be arranged, and the "telephone music" can be recorded on tape for later playback. Each child could determine whether or not his telephone number was "singable." (There are many other criteria to be used in distinguishing melodic from nonmelodic patterns, but this is probably the best place to begin with elementary school children.) Possibly all the "singable" numbers could be recorded on one tape and the "nonsingable" ones on another.

Exploration from this point could take many directions. Individual children may want to experiment with rearranging the sequence of numbers in their telephone number, to see if they can produce a more melodic musical sequence. Small groups of children might work together to compare the melodic and nonmelodic telephone numbers to see if they could identify some characteristics of the melodic sequences. Some children might take a melodic sequence produced by their telephone number and try to extend it to make a song. They would begin to see how brief sequences can be repeated in certain patterns to produce various song forms. Other children might experiment with other kinds of number sequences to see what these produced.

EVALUATION

Can children differentiate between melodic and nonmelodic sequences or patterns?
Can they transform nonmelodic sequences into melodic sequences?
Can they identify some characteristics of melodic sequences?

RELATIONSHIP OF THE LESSON
TO THE TRANSDUCTIVE MODEL

In this lesson children are relating numerical sequences to tonal sequences, thus producing simple musical patterns. They can be relatively objective in evaluating these patterns, because they did not create or invent the patterns themselves.

The process of transforming numbers into notes focuses children's attention on the intervals between musical notes, which is an important element in melodic patterns. In the process children will probably note that a mathematical sequence of whole numbers (1, 2, 3, 4, . . .) has equal intervals between numbers, while the musical sequence of the scale (1, 2, 3, 4, . . . or do, re, mi, fa, . . .) has a set pattern of unequal intervals. The intervals between 3 and 4 (mi-fa) and 7 and 8 (ti-do) are always half tones, and the other intervals are whole tones. Experimentation to produce "singable" sequences gives children an opportunity to develop a basic skill of musical composition, that of arranging notes to create an interesting sequence of sounds.

SAMPLE LESSON IV

OBJECTIVES

To relate visual compositions to musical compositions. To identify elements of composition that are common to both media.

DATA

The teacher will need to supply the data for this lesson. The visual compositions could be four or five pictures representing various styles of art, such as a Jackson Pollack abstract, a Van Gogh landscape, a pop art poster, and a Grant Wood portrait. The musical compositions should also be varied in style—for example, excerpts from the sound track of "2001: A Space Odyssey," a current rock group, a familiar folk song, and "On the Trail" from *The Grand Canyon Suite* by Ferde Grofé.

PROCEDURES

The set of pictures can be set up in front of the room. Children will be told that they will hear a series of short musical passages. They are to decide whether the musical passages fit with any of the pictures.

After each passage is played children can discuss which, if any, of the pictures seem to be similar and in what ways the picture and music are similar. Their comments can be recorded on the board.

There will be no "right" answers in this discussion. Children will probably begin to identify qualities of paintings or music that have not previously occurred to them. For example, a painting and a piece of music may go together because they are both "loud" or because they both use "bright colors."

EVALUATION

Are children able to verbalize relationships between qualities of visual and musical compositions?

RELATIONSHIP OF THE LESSON
TO THE TRANSDUCTIVE MODEL

In this lesson children are being asked to relate visual images to musical images. This process should help to develop new perceptions of techniques used in both forms of composition.

Children might apply these new perceptions by experimenting with the production of loud vs. soft paintings or fast vs. slow paintings or calm vs. excited paintings, depending upon what elements of composition they have identified through their discussion.

INTERACTION IN THE TRANSDUCTIVE LESSON

The lessons above by no means exhaust the possibilities of the transductive discovery model. They are intended only as illustrations of the process of encouraging children to relate two items in order to develop new perceptions of one or both of the items.

Interaction is an important aspect of the transductive lesson. In lessons where the child is working individually to produce a composition the teacher will be interacting with individual children rather than with the whole class at once. The important thing for the teacher to remember is that experimentation by children will be stifled if the teacher begins the lesson by presenting a model (or even various models) to illustrate a possible end-product. As the children's products begin to take shape, however, they can be held up for others to view. This can serve to reward divergent productions, and can stimulate the thinking of other children, as long as a *variety* of children's compositions is used.

In lessons where discussions occur the teacher can follow the same kind of interactive patterns as in the open inductive discovery lesson. Children's ideas should be accepted and if possible recorded for all to consider. The teacher should not make judgments as to their correctness. When pauses occur in the flow of ideas, the teacher must be willing to endure a few moments of silence.

Some teachers will be hesitant to try discovery lessons in the areas of art and music, because they have little background in these areas themselves. There is really little to fear. Children's explorations can produce new insights for the teacher as well as the children. It is not necessary that all of these insights correspond with knowledge already existing in the field. Transductive discovery ought to yield some unique perceptions for all participants.

Self-Evaluation of Learning

The third part of this book has dealt with planning discovery lessons of various types. You may want to check your understanding of this section by completing the following exercise and checking your answers against the answers provided on page 236.

Directions: Given the following sets of teaching objectives, decide what type of discovery lesson (semideductive, structured inductive, open inductive, or transductive) you would plan to use for each set of objectives. You should be able to answer four out of five correctly.

OBJECTIVES—SET I

1. The teacher will introduce the topic of categorization of animals by genus and species
2. The teacher will learn what pupils already know about biological classification systems
3. The teacher will identify the level of classification skills pupils already possess

OBJECTIVES—SET II

1. Pupils will differentiate between adjectives and nouns
2. Pupils will apply their understanding of these differences by generating sentences which use adjectives and nouns in various positions

OBJECTIVES—SET III

1. Pupils will arrive at the generalization that addition is associative, e.g., $(1 + 2) + 5 = 1 + (2 + 5)$

2. Pupils will test to see whether the associative property holds for subtraction as well

OBJECTIVES—SET IV

1. Pupils will generate a number of analogies which could be used to describe a cloudburst
2. Each pupil will apply one of the analogies in writing a poem or drawing a picture about a cloudburst

OBJECTIVES—SET V

1. Pupils will develop the generalization that types of shelter (houses) vary according to the climate and region in which people live
2. Pupils will predict the type of housing they will find in a culture unknown to them, given information about climate and region

PART **IV**

A CHALLENGE
TO MAKE DISCOVERY WORK

Understanding the discovery process and being able to plan various types of discovery lessons are important first steps in meeting the challenge of discovery. They are necessary conditions but they are not sufficient conditions. In this part we shall discuss some of the practical aspects of discovery in action in the classroom. These chapters deal with the problems of insuring successful discovery, using discovery lessons over extended periods of time, making interactive decisions, and managing the classroom for instruction.

chapter **14**

Insuring
Successful Discovery

QUESTIONS TO CONSIDER

Before reading this chapter, try to list at least *two* alternative ways of proceeding in each of the following situations:

    a. Only a few children in the class seem to have any ideas about the generalization, and you are three-quarters of the way through the lesson.

    b. Most of the children in the class seem to have the generalization, but you have just asked Tommy to give you an example that will fit in column 2, and he is unable to answer.

For each of your alternatives, indicate what would be the expected result of this procedure

    1. for the attainment of the generalization;

    2. for the child's or children's self-concept.

We once heard it said by a curriculum specialist that the time will come for some children when it is clear they will not get the generalization on their own but will have to be told. Our response to this is twofold. First, if you believe children learn by being told, then be honest. Tell them and quit wasting time. Second, in a discovery lesson none of the children are really getting the generalization "on their own." The teacher is offering them data and encouragement, and constantly defining their task for them.

We do have several suggestions to make when the class seems to be up against a stone wall or when part of the class is facing the problem of trying to write an accurate generalization and part of the class seems oblivious to what is happening.

The first suggestion is: never hesitate to stop a lesson. It is perfectly legitimate to say to a group of children, "You seem to be stuck here. Let's leave this data on the board until another time. Look at it now and then to see if you can come up with a generalization, but don't fret if you don't get it. Sometimes things need to be left alone for awhile." There are many reasons why children don't see something at a particular moment. All teachers are aware of some of these reasons. We suspect no one is aware of other reasons. It is enough for the teacher that at this moment what he is after isn't being gotten. Let it go and come back later.

The good teacher will in the meantime consider other ways of offering the data and may decide to use another approach. In any event, new approach or old approach, he will come back. It is poor teaching to start to teach a generalization or a way of handling data and to give the whole job up after a few tries. If some of the children have succeeded, then all can succeed. Teachers who devote a week or more to teaching a concept, fail with half the class, and then move on to something else, do considerable damage to the children who fail, and waste a great deal of time because six months or a year later it must be taught again, often to the cry of "we've had this." Further, they fail to grow as teachers. The teacher must continue to pursue the desired ends until they are attained by each child. If it is not attainable by the child, it probably shouldn't have been tried in the first place and the teacher should have known that was the case. Do not move the child from failure to failure. Stay until he succeeds. Success will breed success. Failure will breed failure. Such rejoinders as, "But the curriculum must be covered," are nonsense. A child who fails week after week doesn't cover the curriculum. The difference between teachers covering the curriculum and children covering the curriculum is a big one and an obvious one. Unfortunately, many schools are not run for the benefit of children.

In dealing with children who aren't getting the generalization, you may wish to put the data aside and move to a related lesson in which you use a different set of data. For example, if you were teaching the lesson on short and long vowel sounds described in Chapter 10, and children were having trouble seeing the difference between "hat" and "hate," you might move to a lesson in which you compared "bet" with "beet" and "beat," "set" with "seat," "met" with "meet" and "meat," etc., and try to get the relevant generalizations. Seeing this the children will more than likely see the relationships among the previous data offered. The process of producing a generalization is the same with both sets of data. Once success is gained with one set of data the chances with the second set are increased. Put another way: the more discovery lessons taught, the sooner results are gotten in succeeding lessons.

Let us now look at the problem of the *individual* child who is having trouble forming a generalization.

"IT'S YOUR PROBLEM"

Several years ago one of the authors was teaching a demonstration lesson working with seven youngsters he had met for the first time five minutes earlier. Early in the lesson one child volunteered an incorrect answer and was about to disintegrate into tears when in desperation the teacher said to the boy, "Edward, it's your problem. When you have the correct answer, let us know." The teacher then quickly put another question to the group and called on a volunteer to answer the question. Several other problems similar to the one answered incorrectly were posed by the teacher and answered (correctly) by members of the group. In four or five minutes Edward raised his hand and gave the correct answer to "his" problem. From that point on he volunteered often and was functioning with outstanding success when the lesson ended forty minutes later.

In the past few years we have often thought of Edward and the averted crisis and wondered why the technique of saying to the child, "It's your problem—when you have the correct answer let us know," worked in that instance and in hundreds of instances since. We have come to the conclusion that the technique has a great deal of merit and should be given consideration by other teachers. We should like to discuss here the merits of the technique described above by discussing the consequences of the technique for gaining some of our traditional ends.

Before listing these benefits, it might be well to state some assumptions we hold about the construct, "self-concept." We assume a child's self-concept is revealed by his words and deeds and by his lack of words and deeds. We assume a child who says, "I can," will succeed more often than the child who says, "I can't." We assume that the child who enters into an activity with enthusiasm will get more out of it than the child who hangs back. We assume that success breeds success and failure breeds failure. We do not mean by this that one success or one failure makes any particular difference. We mean, rather, that a pattern of behavior that is success-oriented in an activity such as schooling will tend to lead to more successes in school. School dropouts may leave because they are failing to succeed at age sixteen, but this failure is a result of failing at age fifteen, fourteen, thirteen, on down to age five.

We assume that children derive their self-concepts in part from their perceptions of other people's opinions of them and in part from their own concepts of success and failure.

The technique we have suggested above is related to increasing the probability of turning patterns of failure into patterns of success. The benefits we see following from this technique are several. Briefly stated:

1. A task is clearly defined by the child in a situation that has strong motivating factors operating on the child.
2. When the child is successful, his self-concept is enhanced, in that he has turned failure into success.
3. The child's self-concept is also enhanced in that his classmates have seen him turn failure into success. His peers are usually willing to recognize this success. This recognition tends to strengthen the child's self-concept as a successful problem solver.
4. A number of values are fostered that relate to succeeding in school. Among these are:
   a. Each of us has the right to turn failure into success, rather than to be told by our peers, "You are wrong, you are dumb."
   b. Some people may take more time to solve some problems than other problems. What is important in solving problems is not quickness, but correctness.
   c. When one fails to come up with the correct answer one can still succeed, in that one came to grips with the problem and tried to succeed. In short, the student's responsibility is to try to deal with the problem.
   d. Often the child learns that perseverance can lead to success.

Upon examining point 1, several things seem clearly relevant. Students who offer incorrect answers to questions which are then answered by other students gain little from the situation. Some students who offer incorrect answers tend to offer them again and again. The lesson at any given moment is always just beyond their grasp. Questions asked at the ten-minute mark are often understood later in the lesson but the child has already publicly failed. Repeated public failure leads the child to the belief he is stupid. He may then refuse to participate at all and devote his intelligence to finding ways of nonparticipating or to diverting the class's attention elsewhere.

Many teachers attempt to save the situation by staying with the child and working the problem through with him until he succeeds. The difficulty with this procedure is that the other students are left with little or nothing to do and the child being worked with is operating in a public situation. He will often say, "I can't do it," or intentionally give incorrect answers to get himself off the hook. Being wrong in public is preferable to trying to think on his feet in front of his peers.

There are, of course, teachers who can and do save the situation by staying with the child. There are even those who can make the situation a profitable one for all of the children by introducing new data to the child in difficulty in such a manner as to bring new insights to those who already have the correct answer but who may not fully appreciate why it is the correct answer.

For many teachers, however, the situation cannot be solved this way and they go the alternative of asking if someone else can help out with the correct answer. This practice doesn't help the self-concept of the child who gave the incorrect response. We suspect it is also of little value to the other children, in that they are taught to climb over the dead body of their fallen classmate.

The technique proposed here takes the public pressure off the children in that it says to the class that the problem is no longer available to everyone. It belongs to Eddie, who has volunteered to try to find an answer. Since he has asked, we are obligated under the rules of the class-room to give him all of the time he feels he needs. He is now free to pursue the answer in the way he sees fit, to pursue it privately (thinking being a private matter), and his privacy shall be respected by the group. But further, through this technique the teacher is implicitly stating, "You have given an incorrect answer but if I give you enough time I'm confident you can get the correct answer." The child is thus supported by the teacher and the bond between teacher and student is strengthened. The teacher's role once she has invoked the "It's your problem—let us know when you have the correct answer" technique is to move to a series of similar or related problems that will assist the child in solving his problem and which will enable the teacher to further the knowledge and test the insights of the other youngsters.

It takes little genius to see that the child who fails and later succeeds will have his self-concept enhanced, and we would submit that the longer the time between failure and success, the greater will be the enhancement of the self-concept, if for no other reason than that the reward is greater because success took perseverance as well as insight. It is not being suggested here that long-term failures be built in, but rather that they do sometimes occur and teachers shouldn't be overly concerned. We once asked a youngster we were teaching to produce the logical consequence of $A = B$ and $B = C$. The student was unable to draw the conclusion even though she could see that if two pints equal one quart and one quart equals four cups, then two pints must equal four cups. We would ask every two or three weeks if she had a solution and were repeatedly told no. Four months after the question was first put, we again asked and were told almost casually, with the slightest smile, that $A = C$.

That our self-concepts are a function of how others see us is so axiomatic as to need no supporting evidence here. Others tend to see us largely in terms of how we perform. If we fail and fail again, others tend to see us as failures. If, however, we can succeed repeatedly, we are seen as being successful and consequently begin to believe it ourselves. A very successful teacher in remedial work once told us that the job was a simple one. "You need only change 'I can't' into 'I can' to get a complete metamorphosis" is the way this teacher put it. The technique suggested here helps insure all of the above. By leaving the problem temporarily unanswered and making it the responsibility of one child, you head off the immediate failure; and the student's classmates must withhold the judgment that he failed. When the correct answer finally is offered, the peer group must acknowledge success, for even if they also recognize that their classmate was a little slow in getting the answer, he did get it. Slow or not, he persevered.

On occasion we have posed problems at the end of a lesson which we felt reasonably confident no one in the group could answer without prolonged cogitation. On some of these occasions the child judged to be the slowest got the correct answer first. The impact on the class is something to behold. The children are not resentful, but enthusiastic in their praise; and the face of the so-called slow child is a beautiful thing to see. Indeed, in the next lesson a stranger would be hardput to guess that this child whom the others are listening to with such respect is the "class dummy." We should perhaps note that teachers are sometimes discouraging at these moments of success. While the child's classmates offer praise and alter their view of their peer, teachers will often suggest that the child made a lucky guess and will continue to view the child as stupid. Such self-confirming hypotheses can prove harmful to children and frustrate successful teaching.

Much has been said about teaching values. Much more has been done in preaching values. We are convinced that values are "deutero learning," to use Honigmann's term. They are learned unconsciously. Words about respecting each other and each other's rights are meaningless unless consistent with action. Further, if our actions as teachers respect children and the rights of children, then few words are needed. The lesson will be learned. To teach values effectively, then, we need to examine values as they are reflected in our techniques. If one examines the technique proposed strictly from an ethical standpoint, several considerations come to mind. Our job as teachers is to produce successful scholars. Our job is to uphold and foster the dignity of the individual. In order to attain the second objective, practices that give equal treatment to the child who is slow to come to a conclusion are essential. Every opportunity must be given the child so that he may succeed with dignity.

Many teachers who ask children for quick answers in pressure-packed situations that lead to repeated public failures and demoralization will sit in graduate courses and be highly resentful if asked by education professors why they think they are entitled to a minimum salary of $7,000 or what did Dewey mean on such and such a point. If a child volunteers to help us teach a lesson by making public his private judgment on a question, should we not respect this judgment in action as well as in words? The child, when he volunteers, has indicated a willingness to deal with our problem, to make our problem his problem. Have we a right to take away this problem and give it to another child?

Judge if you will the hypothetical teacher in the following story. At playtime in a kindergarten class a teacher holds up a jigsaw puzzle and asks who would like to try to put this puzzle together. Six hands go up and the teacher says, "Here, Mary, you try the puzzle." Mary spreads out the pieces of the puzzle and tries to fit two pieces together and doesn't succeed. The teacher then says "Who would like to help Mary? She is unable to put the puzzle together." Getting a volunteer, the teacher takes the puzzle from Mary and gives it to another student.

From an ethical standpoint, what is the difference in volunteering to answer a question or to do a puzzle? Among other things, most of us would probably say to our hypothetical colleague: "Why are you hostile toward Mary? She volunteers to cooperate with you by doing the puzzle and you hold her up to public ridicule. Don't you realize that it is the process of solving the problem that is important. It is in the solving process that most of the learning takes place. As a teacher you have failed by denying Mary an opportunity to learn."

Our ethics as teachers are such that we are bound to create and foster learning situations and to involve children in these learning situations. Furthermore, it is through involving children in learning situations in which they succeed that we hope to bring them to the view that they can succeed as learners and that learning is a valuable and satisfying experience. Again, what is the difference in volunteering to answer a question or to do a puzzle? Are not all the same variables at work? Are not the goals the same?

Our first job, we have said, was to produce successful scholars. Scholarship is, however, a function of values. Commitment to learning is essential to scholarship. Commitment to truth is necessary to scholarship. Willingness to withhold judgment is necessary. Recognition that truth is not always a matter of authority but a function of the intellectual rules of the game (the game being either math, history, science, etc.) is necessary. Perseverance is necessary. Humility is necessary. We should like to argue that using the "It's your problem" technique once will not develop any of the values stated above, but that repeated use, day in and day out, will.

The child who fails on a particular question and then solves it and fails on another and then solves it, and occasionally fails altogether, is learning to persevere, to be humble, to withhold judgment. He is learning that scholarship is a series of challenges. They are challenges only because he has failed to find an answer. He is learning that once the challenge is met another presents itself. He will have finally learned that life, like scholarship, consists of facing a series of challenges. Some of them he will meet successfully and take strength from. Some of them he will not meet successfully. But he can take satisfaction in the knowledge that he gave his best, because that will be his self-concept.

chapter **15**

Teaching by Discovery
Over Extended Periods of Time

A single discovery lesson of the type described in the foregoing chapters can be fun for both the teacher and the pupils if it provides a break in the classroom routine of prescriptive lessons, workbook pages, or programmed instructional materials. But an isolated discovery lesson will never provide the really important payoff. If your end is to help children to become independent thinkers and problem solvers, then discovery lessons must proceed over longer periods of time. A problem must be wrestled with day after day. A pet solution must be seen to be inadequate. Generalizations must be revised to fit new evidence.

In teaching children to revise generalizations and identify new problems it is frequently useful to begin working with a topic that is not generally part of the regular curriculum. Most teachers will find it easier to let children explore, work for a while with inadequate generalizations, and propose divergent solutions or procedures if the teacher is not under any pressure to have children "know" a particular answer at a particular point in the school year.

We find the lattice to be a very useful topic for this purpose. It is a mathematical system that can be explored productively by children in the first grade and by graduate students in college, so it can be used at any grade level in the elementary school. The lattice can lead to the exploration of many areas of mathematics, so it lends itself to work over extended periods of time. In the pages which follow we shall suggest several of the many possible ways of using a lattice to encourage children to become independent problem solvers.

TEACHING A LATTICE

```
40

30  31  32  33  34  35  36  37  38  39

20  21  22  23  24  25  26  27  28  29

10  11  12  13  14  15  16  17  18  19

 0   1   2   3   4   5   6   7   8   9
```

Fig. 15–1

Figure 15–1 shows a lattice. One strategy for introducing work with a lattice is to display the lattice on the board, to write the following problem on the board:

$$12\uparrow =$$

and ask, "What do you think is the answer to this problem?"

Another strategy is to write the following on the board.

22 → = 23	12 → = 13	25 ↑ =
15 ↓ = 5	17 ↗ = 28	19 ↓ =
17 ↙ = 6	28 ↗ =	39 ↙ =
12 ↑ =	3 → =	15 ↗ =
12 ← = 11	4 ← =	3 → =
	3 ← = 2	

When the correct answers have been filled in the teacher may ask, "How many more are there?" Several answers are possible. The most general one given is two more: ↖ and ↘. Sometimes a child will say, "Many more," and demonstrate as shown in Fig. 15–2.

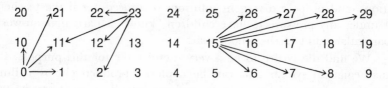

Fig. 15–2

Indeed, one fourth-grade boy once argued that an infinite number of arrows could be drawn from 15 to each number ending in 9, an infinite number of arrows from 15 to the 8s column, an infinite number of arrows from 15 to the 7s column, and so forth, giving a total of 4 times infinity to the right of 15 and 5 times infinity to the left of 15. This makes for a lot of arrows and a number of interesting problems which we shall not pursue here.

If the above is explored, one can then come back and settle for the eight arrows ↑, ↗, →, ↘, ↓, ↙, ←, ↖, but even that isn't necessary. If the children say they don't know how many arrows there are, the teacher may simply note the question on the side of the board, observing that when someone knows the answer they can write it down. The view here is that the art of teaching is more a case of getting the question before the class than of getting the answer. The answer will come soon enough, and it should come from the data and the children, not from the teacher.

The next strategy may be to ask the answers to the following:

$$16 ↑ → → \quad = 28$$
$$17 → → → \quad =$$
$$18 ↑ ↑ ↖ \quad =$$
$$22 ↑ → \quad =$$
$$15 ↑ → ↓ → ↑ =$$
etc.

This may be handled by giving some answers and should be continued until everyone is getting the correct answers. Longer problems may also be offered.

The problem 21 ↑ → → ↑ → ↓ ↙ ↙ ← ↑ → = _____ is one children enjoy very much. It is a good idea at this point to give children a copy of the lattice so that they may pursue the answer with a pencil or their fingers. Errors in longer problems which must be solved at a distance are more likely to be due to visual difficulties rather than intellectual ones.

A good strategy at this point is to ask children to do the following problem:

$$12 \qquad\qquad = 27$$

The result will be a wide variety of answers. The minimum number of arrows will be five, the maximum is restricted only by the condition that the statement must be completed. Some children recognize in doing these problems that there are an infinite number of ways of getting from one number to the number next to it.

When this is seen, restrictions may be put on the way children operate. For example, (1) get from 13 to 27 using five arrows and never go above the 20s line; (2) find all the ways you can of getting from 13 to

27, using no more than four arrows; (3) find the shortest route (or minimum number of arrows) between 13 and 27; (4) find the minimum number of arrows necessary to get from 13 to 27 when no arrow moves obliquely.

Logical permutations are used to solve these problems. If we must find all of the ways of getting from 15 to 28 using three arrows we get:

$$15 \nearrow \rightarrow \rightarrow = 28$$
$$15 \rightarrow \nearrow \rightarrow = 28$$
$$15 \rightarrow \rightarrow \nearrow = 28$$
$$15 \nearrow \nearrow \searrow = 28$$
$$15 \nearrow \searrow \nearrow = 28$$
$$15 \searrow \nearrow \nearrow = 28$$

In going from 15 to 37 we get:

$$15 \uparrow \rightarrow \nearrow = 37$$
$$15 \uparrow \nearrow \rightarrow = 37$$
$$15 \rightarrow \nearrow \uparrow = 37$$
$$15 \rightarrow \uparrow \nearrow = 37$$
$$15 \nearrow \uparrow \rightarrow = 37$$
$$15 \nearrow \rightarrow \uparrow = 37$$

In going from 15 to 28 we found six ways of going, using three different arrows ($\rightarrow \nearrow \searrow$). The same is true of going from 15 to 37. But in going from 15 to 28 we only used two different arrows in each problem ($\nearrow$ and $\rightarrow$, or $\nearrow$ and $\searrow$), and the two arrows could be used three different ways. In getting from 15 to 37 three different arrows were used in each problem ($\uparrow$, $\rightarrow$, and $\nearrow$) but there were six different ways of using them.

QUESTIONS TO CONSIDER

Can you explain how to predict the number of possible ways of getting from one number to another in the above examples?

Would the children in your class have to know the rule for logical permutations in order to generate all the possible ways of getting from one number to another?

The problem of generating logical permutations of a set of arrows points up the fact that different children can work on the same problem at different levels. Some children in a class will generate different arrangements of arrows in haphazard or random ways, but they can solve the problem by simply moving the arrows around. Other children may face the logical problem of figuring out how many possibilities there ought to be. Some children will combine logical and random strategies— for example, using commutativity as a means of rearranging some arrows and doing others randomly. All of the children are dealing with the problem at their own level of understanding or cognitive development.

REVISING INADEQUATE GENERALIZATIONS

Another example of this same phenomenon of individual differences can be seen when the problem of alternating arrows is introduced to children. The teacher's objective is to get children to work at continually revising and improving their generalization. One's strategy might be to offer the following problems one at a time:

$$8 \uparrow\downarrow\uparrow\downarrow\uparrow\downarrow\uparrow\downarrow =$$
$$22 \uparrow\downarrow\uparrow\downarrow\uparrow\downarrow\uparrow\downarrow =$$
$$14 \uparrow\downarrow\uparrow\downarrow\uparrow\downarrow\uparrow\downarrow =$$
$$29 \uparrow\downarrow\uparrow\downarrow\uparrow\downarrow\uparrow\downarrow =$$
$$33 \uparrow\downarrow\uparrow\downarrow\uparrow\downarrow\uparrow\downarrow =$$
$$\text{etc.}$$

Children will at first handle these by following each arrow on the lattice. Then some will begin to see that the alternating arrows are having the opposite effect, in that they cancel each other out, and they will begin to get the answer very quickly. At this point many will be able to produce the generalization, "Alternating up and down arrows bring you back to the same point." The teacher may then offer:

$$21 \uparrow\downarrow\uparrow\downarrow\uparrow\downarrow\uparrow\downarrow\uparrow =$$

The answer is, of course, 31. The procedure is consistent with the generalization and yet one doesn't end at the same place. The generalization may then be modified to read, "When you have an even number of alternating up and down arrows, you end at the starting point; if you have an odd number of alternating arrows, you end at a point immediately above your starting place."

The teacher then offers:

$$16 \downarrow\uparrow\downarrow\uparrow\downarrow\uparrow\downarrow\uparrow\downarrow =$$

This time the second half of the generalization may be altered to read ". . . if you have an odd number of alternating arrows, your first and last arrow will indicate whether you finish immediately above or below your last arrow."

The teacher may then offer:

$$21 \nearrow \swarrow \nearrow \swarrow \nearrow \swarrow =$$

in order to knock "up and down" out of the generalization. What will happen at this point is that many if not all children will go back to handling one arrow at a time until they see that $\nearrow \swarrow \nearrow \swarrow$ is also an alternating phenomenon. Some children will at this point produce another generalization for oblique arrows and have two generalizations, one relating to oblique arrows and one relating to up and down arrows. Others will try to write one generalization that covers both types of arrows. The second, is, of course, the intellectual ideal as it is more economical in terms of words. The second strategy also gives one a generalization that covers more data.

The teacher may now offer problems like the following:

$$15 \rightarrow \leftarrow \rightarrow \leftarrow \rightarrow \leftarrow =$$
$$21 \searrow \nwarrow \searrow \nwarrow \searrow \nwarrow =$$
$$33 \searrow \nwarrow \searrow \nwarrow \searrow \nwarrow \searrow =$$

Enough of each should be given until most of the children are getting the answers rapidly and are able to develop a set of generalizations to explain the shortcuts being taken.

Several points should be noted here. First, all children who were able to solve the first multiple-arrow problems can solve all of those above by moving on the lattice one arrow at a time. Consequently, all of the children will get the correct answers to the problems posed. Some children, however, will perceive the logical problem, thereby recognizing that the problem can be handled intellectually without operating directly on the lattice. Some will attempt to construct a different generalization for each type of problem (up-down arrows, oblique arrows, opposing arrows) while others will be facing the single, more complicated problem of finding one generalization that applies to all of these problems. This group has recognized that all of these problems are of one type: each has alternating arrows.

The next strategy can be to offer the following type of problem:

$$17 \uparrow \uparrow \uparrow \downarrow \downarrow \downarrow =$$
$$29 \downarrow \downarrow \downarrow \downarrow \uparrow \uparrow \uparrow \uparrow =$$
$$32 \nearrow \nearrow \nearrow \swarrow \swarrow \swarrow \nearrow \swarrow =$$

In these the whole notion of alternating goes out the window. If the teacher then provides the following problems to be solved:

$$25 \uparrow \nearrow \downarrow \swarrow \nearrow \downarrow \uparrow \swarrow =$$
$$13 \uparrow \uparrow \swarrow \swarrow \downarrow \downarrow \nearrow \nearrow =$$
$$31 \rightarrow \leftarrow \uparrow \downarrow \nearrow \swarrow \searrow \nwarrow =$$

The notion of the two opposing arrows falls. It is still possible to solve these problems logically by comparing the number of up and down arrows and the number of left and right arrows. In $25 \uparrow \nearrow \downarrow \swarrow \nearrow \downarrow \uparrow \swarrow$ = _____ arrows 1, 2, 5, and 7 go up and are cancelled by arrows 3, 4, 6, and 8. Arrows 2 and 5 go right and are cancelled by 4 and 8.

At this stage of the game, many of the children who were looking for logical shortcuts earlier will be back to handling the arrows one at a time on the lattice, and even those who have found a logical means of handling these problems will often check their work by moving one arrow at a time. Some children will handle part of the problem logically and the rest one at a time on the lattice. Again using the problem $25 \uparrow \nearrow \downarrow \swarrow \nearrow \downarrow \uparrow \swarrow$ = _____, some children may immediately eliminate arrows 6 and 7 because they see that they cancel and then proceed to handle the rest one at a time. Others will see that 4 and 5 also cancel, thus handling 4, 5, 6, and 7 logically, and proceed to handle the rest on the lattice. In making these logical moves they are applying principles they developed earlier.

If the teacher poses the task of finding the time-saving device of using logical moves rather than physical moves and gives the children enough opportunities, they will all learn to function quite effectively. We once observed a first-grade class after a week's practice that could handle problems with thirty arrows as quickly as the teacher could write them on the board.

POSING MORE DIFFICULT PROBLEMS

The problem can be further complicated by offering a series of problems paired as follows:

$15 \uparrow \rightarrow$ =	$22 \uparrow \rightarrow$ =	$13 \uparrow \rightarrow$ =
$15 \nearrow$ =	$22 \nearrow$ =	$13 \nearrow$ =
$48 \uparrow \rightarrow$ =	$72 \uparrow \rightarrow$ =	
$48 \nearrow$ =	$72 \nearrow$ =	

Then offer the following:

$$\uparrow \rightarrow \ =$$

Now, the answer desired is $\uparrow \rightarrow \ = \ \nearrow$, but children will say, "11," and stop looking for another answer. The cure here is to construct a situation where $\uparrow \rightarrow$ doesn't equal 11. This is done by putting the following on the board:

$$
\begin{array}{ccc}
g & h & i \\
d & e & f \\
a & b & c
\end{array}
$$

Then ask the answer to $b \uparrow \rightarrow \ = \ _____$. The children see that the answer is f and that the difference between b and f is not 11. One can then ask the answer to $b \nearrow \ = \ _____$, and again the answer will be f. Eventually, with enough examples (and sometimes the teacher must offer similar but different problems, such as $20 \nearrow \downarrow \ = \ _____$, $20 \rightarrow \ =$ $_____$, $7 \uparrow \leftarrow \ = \ _____$, $7 \nwarrow \ = \ _____$), the children see that $\uparrow \rightarrow \ = \ \nearrow$. The teacher may then move to the following kinds of problems:

$$
\begin{array}{lll}
15 \rightarrow \uparrow \ = & 20 \nearrow \quad = & 16 \rightarrow \uparrow \ = \\
15 \nearrow \quad = & 20 \rightarrow \uparrow \ = & 16 \nearrow \quad =
\end{array}
$$

Children will soon see that $\nearrow \ = \ \rightarrow \uparrow$. We now have:

$$
\uparrow \rightarrow \ = \ \nearrow \\
\nearrow \ = \ \rightarrow \uparrow
$$

and can pose the following problem:

"Can you construct a third true statement which logically follows from these two. You must use both statements to produce your third statement."

The latter is necessary as some children will observe that $\nearrow \ = \ \uparrow \rightarrow$, which is true and which follows from $\uparrow \rightarrow \ = \ \nearrow$. However, it follows from only one statement, not two. What we are after is:

$$
\uparrow \rightarrow \ = \ \nearrow \\
\nearrow \ = \ \rightarrow \uparrow \\
\uparrow \rightarrow \ = \ \rightarrow \uparrow
$$

If one labels $\uparrow \rightarrow a$, $\nearrow b$, and $\rightarrow \uparrow c$ we have:

$$a = b$$
$$b = c$$
$$\therefore a = c$$

Equals being equal to equals are equal.

The syllogism is not easy to get at first, for $\uparrow \rightarrow = \nearrow$ is more diffi-cult than doing problems that yield a specific number representing a point in space. Examining the relationship of $\uparrow \rightarrow = \nearrow$ to $\nearrow = \rightarrow \uparrow$ is still more difficult, but it is well worth going after, as it goes to the heart of logical reasoning.

An eight-year-old once held at the twenty-five-minute mark of a les-son that if $a = b$ and $b = c$, then $a = c$. She couldn't explain why, but felt strongly enough about it to stand alone when all of her classmates disagreed. At the forty-minute mark of the lesson the teacher, working with other arrows, had on the board $m = n$ and $n = p$. Half the class now concluded that m must equal p. Our eight-year-old girl was asked what she thought and she replied as follows: "I don't believe m must equal p because m equals n and n equals p, but I still believe that a must equal c in the earlier problem. But I'm worried because if a equals c, then m must equal p. Either both are true or both are false. I'm not sure."

Perhaps she wasn't sure of that particular answer, but she was gaining an appreciation of a phenomenon called "logical necessity."

A postscript to this anecdote: one young man (nine years old) who failed to see that a must equal c and m equal p approached his teacher two months after the lesson and showed the teacher his worksheet, which had the following on it:

$$0 + 5 = 5$$
$$1 + 4 = 5$$
$$2 + 3 = 5$$
$$3 + 2 = 5$$
$$4 + 1 = 5$$
$$5 + 0 = 5$$

He then observed, "Look, if you rearrange any of these two prob-lems you get $a = b$, $b = c$; therefore, $a = c$. If $0 + 5 = 5$ and $5 = 1 + 4$, then $0 + 5$ must equal $1 + 4$."

Again we note that the job of the teacher is to get the question before the child. If it's a legitimate question, it will come up again and again, each time to be puzzled over anew, until it is finally solved. Different children will solve it at different points in time, as the above examples indicate. This is preferable to having the teacher "solve" it for everyone at the same time. It is also preferable to avoiding all difficult questions.

ALTERNATIVE METHODS FOR SOLVING PROBLEMS ON THE LATTICE

Once the children see that $\uparrow \rightarrow \ = \ \nearrow$, they are quick to see that $\uparrow \rightarrow$ is cancelled out by $\swarrow$ as effectively as $\uparrow$ cancels out $\downarrow$. The whole notion of an even number of arrows now goes by the board.

Problems such as

$$15 \uparrow \leftarrow \uparrow \rightarrow \swarrow \searrow \ =$$

are solved through recognizing that the last two arrows have the opposite effect of the first four arrows. Arrow 6 cancels out arrows 1 and 2 and arrow 5 cancels out arrows 3 and 4. The handling of these examples presents a real problem. In

the example is handled by circling opposites and connecting them. The same problems may, of course, be handled in less sophisticated ways:

But circling is not the only way to handle these problems. Some children invent a numbering system in which we have four possible values. We might call these $+N$, $-N$, $+E$, and $-E$, with N standing for north and E for east. Thus a $\uparrow$ is $+N$ while $\downarrow$ is $-N$. A $\rightarrow$ would be $+E$ and $\leftarrow$ would be $-E$. The method then goes like this

$$25 \uparrow \rightarrow \rightarrow \leftarrow \downarrow \downarrow \uparrow \leftarrow \leftarrow \uparrow \ =$$

Count the $+N$s; there are 3. Count the $-N$s; there are 3—therefore, they cancel out the $+N$s. Count the $+E$s; there are 2. Count the $-E$s; there are 3, which is greater than 2 by 1. The answer is therefore 24. Some label the Ns "V" for vertical, and the Es "H" for horizontal. Thus with a $-H$ we know that the H means we move horizontally and the minus sign means to move to the left.

The arrows $\nearrow$, $\swarrow$, $\searrow$, $\nwarrow$, have two values: $\nearrow$ gives us a $+V$ and a $+H$, while $\nwarrow$ gives us a $+V$ and a $-H$; $\searrow$ is a $-V$ and a $+H$. Children will again handle these differently. Examine the following problem·

55 ↑ ↗ ↓ → ↙ ↙ ↖ ↑ ↓ → ↙ ↑ ↘ ← ← ↘ ↑ → → =

By counting quickly all arrows that point up we get +6V. By counting all that point down we get −7V. Adding up, we get −1V and know our answer lies in the 40s. The arrows that point right (2, 4, 10, 13, 16, 18, and 19) give us +7H. Arrows 5, 6, 7, 11, 14, and 15 point left, giving us a −6H. A +7H and a −6H adds up to a +1H and we know therefore that our answer ends in 6. Therefore our answer is 46.

Some children handle the above problem in two steps. They first handle the vertical, starting at the left with arrow 1, which gives that a +1; arrow 2 makes it +2 while 3 makes it +1 again; 4 is irrelevant; arrows 5 and 6 move us to −1; arrows 7 and 8 move us back to +1; arrow 9 moves us to zero; etc. Children will, of course, learn to do this quite quickly. Some develop the ability to handle both V and H simultaneously. Thus arrow 1 is 1V and 0H; arrow 2 moves us to 2V and 1H; arrow 3 moves us to 1V and 1H; arrow 4 leaves us at 1V and moves us to 2H; arrow 5 moves us to 0V and 1H, arrow 6 to −1V and 0H, arrow 7 to 0V and −1H, arrow 8 to 1V and −1H, arrow 9 to 0V and −1H, and arrow 10 to 0V and 0H; arrow 11 moves us to −1V and −1H, and 12 takes us to 0V and −1H, arrow 13 to −1V and 0H, 14 to −1V and −1H, 15 to −1V and −2H, 16 to −2V and −1H, 17 to −1V and −1H, 18 to −1V and 0H, and 19 to −1V and +1H.

The solution of the problem in the manner suggested above is fairly sophisticated, but can be handled by children. It should be noted, however, that even this problem can be solved by a child handling one arrow at a time on the lattice. And children who have developed fairly sophisticated means of handling the problem quickly may not be able to handle all of the means at this point. It is an interesting phenomenon that children, like adults, will fall back on the tried and true methods when they get into difficulty with new methods. There is no harm done by this strategy. The harm is done when this strategy is reinforced with praise. Let the child go back to the tried and true, but encourage him and others to keep seeking the big generalizations; and don't accept the job as completed until they have each found the big generalization.

DEVELOPING CHILDREN'S INDEPENDENCE

We indicated earlier in the lesson that different children will be facing different problems of different complexities all at the same time in the same lesson. Lessons that are built this way lead to a much more efficient and effective handling of individual differences. They also lead to more independence on the part of the thinking child. Note that when we first offered problems like 22 $\uparrow\downarrow\uparrow\uparrow\downarrow\uparrow\uparrow\downarrow$ we didn't ask the children to find a shortcut or to generalize about up and down arrows. They saw the problem and tackled it. A second-grade girl looked at the first two-arrow problem, which was 14 $\uparrow\rightarrow$, and volunteered to her teacher that $\uparrow\rightarrow = \nearrow$ "and there must be more of these." The teacher asked if she wished to pursue it and the girl said yes. She tuned out on the lesson and forty minutes later reported there were sixteen statements where two arrows equal one, and eight statements where two different arrows equaled two of the same kind (e.g., $\nearrow\searrow = \rightarrow\rightarrow$).

What happens in good discovery teaching, then, is that the teacher offers to the children a great deal of data which have buried in them a series of problems. Once the child discovers that something is amiss or has an insight that would explain the data or reveal some of its truth, the teacher should get out of the way and let the child pursue his insights. Often children will see things that the teacher missed, as in the case of the child who saw four infinities to the right and five to the left. The attempt to find solutions to self-discovered problems leads to other problems, such as: How do I proceed? and What is relevant here? The situation is a true problem situation and has in it all the ingredients that face any scholar: data, previous knowledge, a problematical situation, a relevant factual situation, anxiety, methodological problems, logical problems, the need for care and rigor, etc. It is in these situations that children learn to learn. As the children produce generalizations from these problematical situations and offer them as truth, the teacher adds new data or presents the data already available so that it is seen differently by the child, and the inadequacy of the child's generalization is seen or its adequacy is more fully appreciated. When enough of his generalizations fall in this manner the child will eventually come to appreciate the difficulty of quick answers and begin to develop techniques or strategies to insure the worth of his generalizations. Truth, he learns, is hard to come by and comes in different forms with differing degrees of certainty. In all of this he rarely receives the response of "Right" or "Wrong" from the teacher. Truth, unfortunately—or perhaps fortunately—is now seen by the child as resting on grounds other than that "the teacher says so."

The interactive pattern, then, of discovery teaching is as follows:

1. Teacher offers data.
2. Child responds to data and comes to a conclusion.
3. Teacher offers new data or presents data in a different form that will cause child to test his conclusion and to validate it, extend it, modify it, or reject it.

4. Child validates conclusion, modifies it, extends it, or rejects it and develops new conclusion.
5. Teacher offers new or reorganized data again.
6. Child validates or modifies again.

This pattern is repeated until the child begins to search for new data or reorganizations that may or may not lead to a modification of conclusions. At this point the child is not only searching for the correct conclusion but for the correct means or strategies that will insure that a conclusion reached is correct. At this point the teacher moves into the background. The child becomes independent enough to search out his own new data in order to test his conclusion.

ADDITIONAL USES OF THE LATTICE

To return to the lattice for a moment, let us note that there are a number of other problems one can pose to children using the lattice that call for them to agree upon what is allowable and what isn't. For instance, $6 \downarrow \uparrow \uparrow = \underline{\quad}$ is no problem when handled logically. Moving step-by-step on the lattice, however, it is impossible unless one introduces negative numbers. As another example, $19 \rightarrow = \underline{\quad}$ also offers a challenge to the solver. The children must decide what rules they will establish for the system, and determine where those rules will lead.

One teacher we observed used a lattice to teach negative numbers. This teacher used the 10s column as a number line and defined moving up the columns as $+$ and moving down as $-$. This was done by first using the following kind of notation:

$$30 + (2\uparrow) + (1\downarrow) = 40, \qquad 20 + (5\uparrow) + (6\downarrow) = 10$$

Then the problems were changed to read:

$$30 + [2 \times (+10)] + [1 \times (-10)] =$$

and

$$20 + [5 \times (+10)] + [6 \times (-10)] =$$

The problems were extended from this to problems of the following type:

$$20 + 3[5 \times (+10)] + 2[6 \times (-10)] =$$

Many of the children at this point were no longer using the lattice to get their answers. This teacher eventually got to the rules that govern multiplying negative × negative, negative × positive, and positive × positive. She had a "slow" fourth grade. That is, they were labeled "slow." One of the benefits of encouraging children to think for themselves is that they frequently learn more by solving their own problems than most teachers would dare to try to teach them.

chapter **16**

Making Interactive Decisions

Planning discovery lessons is only one part of the process of teaching by discovery. As we have noted in several chapters, the interaction between the teacher and the children in the actual lesson is the most crucial part of discovery teaching.

It is difficult to provide practice in interactive skills through the medium of a book, but we have attempted to simulate the problem of interactive decision making in the following exercise. Discussing the decision you are asked to make with classmates later should help to point up important principles of the interactive process.

ASSIGNMENT

In this exercise you will be provided with a partial transcript of a lesson being taught to a group of children. At the point when the transcript stops, the teacher is expected to make some sort of response to the situation.

Study the lesson plan carefully so you know what you, as the teacher, are trying to teach. When you are ready, take *five minutes* to read the transcript, decide what you would do next as the teacher, and indicate that response in writing. That is, explain what you would do, or what you would ask the children, or what you would tell the children at this point in the lesson and how you would then proceed to end the lesson.

LESSON PLAN

OBJECTIVES

1. Pupils will state that the *er* ending is used to change verbs to nouns and also to form the comparative ending of adjectives

2. Pupils will apply a test to determine whether a word ending in *er* is a noun or an adjective

3. Pupils will gain additional skill in using the discovery method

MATERIALS

Worksheets with lists of words as follows:

List One	List Two
work	worker
silly	sillier
run	runner
help	helper
fast	faster
sing	singer
fight	fighter
happy	happier
short	shorter
fat	fatter

PROCEDURES

1. Have children compare list one and list two. Ask: How are they different?

2. Ask if the words in list two are all the same kind of word because they all end the same way?

3. Give children sentence patterns to test words in list two. Write on blackboard:

A	B
1. He can _____.	1. He is very _____.
2. He is a good _____.	2. He is _____ than I am.

Have children try to fit list-one words in sentence 1 in each column and to fit list-two words in sentence 2 in each column. If they fit in the "A" sentences, put them in list A. If they fit in the "B" sentences, put them in list B.

4. Have children use tests they have learned previously to decide what kinds of words they have in list A and list B.

5. Ask children what an *er* ending can tell them about a word.

Give children a worksheet with several sentences. Have them underline the words with *er* endings and decide whether each one is an adjective or a noun.

LANGUAGE ARTS LESSON

T: (*Teacher*): All right. We're going to look at some words today. I have two lists of words for you to look at. I want you to read them over and see what you can tell me about the two lists of words.

(*Children read the following lists:*)

List One	List Two
work	worker
silly	sillier
run	runner
help	helper
fast	faster
sing	singer
fight	fighter
happy	happier
short	shorter
fat	fatter

T: Got some ideas? Jane, what?

Jane: That they all end with *er*, and they mean more?

T: Well, all of the words in which list end in *er*?

Jane: Number two.

T: List two. Okay. Do you notice anything else about either of those lists?

Joe: Well, you have, like, "fat," "fatter"—like, what happens later on.

T: Oh. You think the words in list one are somehow like the words in list two. Is that what you mean, Joe?

Joe: Uh huh.

T: How are they different?

Ruth: Well, you have "work." "Work" is like when you are writing something down, and you have to do it. "Worker" is a *person* who has to do it.

T: Very good. Now you've said there are some differences between list one and list two, and there are some ways in which the words in list two are alike. Right?

Children: Yes.

T: Do you think all the words in list two are the same kind of word?

Ira: No.

T: You don't. Do you, Jane?

Jane: No.

T: Why not?

Jane: 'Cause like "fat," then "fatter." They're different.

T: Well, which word is in list two?

Jane: "Fatter."

T: All right. Now look at the words in list two, and forget about the words in list one for a minute. Tell me, do you think that all the words in list two are the same kind of word? You said they all end in *er*. (*Children study lists.*)

Joe: Well, you would say that these are more of an action word.

T: You think the words in list two are action words. Do you agree with him, Ira?

Ira: Yes.

T: And do you think *all* the words in list two are action words?

Jane: In list two?

T: Yes.

Jane: Yes, I think so.

Ruth: Well, I don't consider "shorter" an action word.

T: You think maybe some of them aren't action words?

(*Joe nods agreement.*)

T: But you think most of them are?

Joe: Yes. Most of them are.

The transcription is interrupted here. What would you, as the teacher, do next?

COMPARING DECISIONS

When you have written your response to the partial transcript (the interactive teaching decision), compare your decision to those of others in your group. What effect does each decision have upon the probable attainment of objectives? Which objective has become most important to you as the teacher? Why is this objective most important to you? (Write your answer briefly.)

After comparing your decision with those of your classmates, you may want to read a transcript of the rest of the lesson, and compare that teacher's decision with your own. The transcript follows. Please control your curiosity until after your discussion.

LANGUAGE ARTS LESSON (cont.)

T: All right. I'm going to give you something to do to check and see whether you're right that there are more than one kind of word in list two. But first I'd like you to make me two groups of words from list two. You already said there are some action words and some words that aren't action words. I want each of you to put the words that you think are action words in one group, and the words that you think are not action words in another group.

So down at the bottom of your paper let's make a list called "X" and a list called "Y." Under "X" you list the words you think are action words, and under "Y" you list the words you think are something else.

Jane: You mean words from both of these lists?

T: No, just the words from list two. We'll forget about list one for a minute.

Ira: What are the action words again?

T: "X" is the group for action words. "X" for action.

(*Children make lists.*)

Ira: What's "Y" for? The ones that aren't action words?

T: Yes. That's right. Action words under "X" and the other words under "Y."

(*Children continue to make lists.*)

Ira: What's this word?

T: "Sillier."

(*Children continue to make lists.*)

T: Are you all done, Ruth?

Ruth: Uh huh.

T: Good. Let's wait just a minute until the others are finished. Now are we all done?

(*Children nod.*)

T: All right. Joe, will you read your list "X"?

Joe: "Worker," "runner," "helper," "faster," "singer," "sillier," "fighter."

T: And you think all those are action words. Now read your list "Y."

Joe: "Happier," "shorter," and "fatter."

T: And those are not action words. So that's the way you would divide them. Now, Ira, let's see if you agree with Joe. You read your action words.

Ira: "Worker," "happier," "runner," "helper," "faster," "shorter," "singer," and "fatter."

T: Those are action words, you think. And what about your list of words that aren't action words?

Ira: "Sillier" and "frightened."

T: "Fighter," that word is.

Ira: Oh. "Fighter."

T: "Sillier" and "fighter." Now did you two agree on your lists?

Ira: I think Joe's right.

T: Why do you think that he's right?

Ruth: Well, is "fatter" really an action word?

Jane: "Fatter"—you get fatter right there and then.

Ira: No. "Fatter," it takes a long time to do it. And "shorter," it takes a long time. And "worker."

T: How many people agree with Joe's list?

(*No hands raised.*)

T: How many agree with Ira's list?

(*No hands raised.*)

T: How many have a different list?

(*Two hands raised.*)

T: Well, we all seem to disagree. Your groups of action words are not the same. Do you think you might have some mistakes in yours, Ira?

Ira: Yes.

T: Joe, do you think your group "X" is right, now?

Joe: Well, there might be one wrong.

T: Okay. Now I'm going to give you something to make two lists again, but to do it another way. We'll see if you end up with the same thing this time.

Now we have some sentences here.

(*T writes on the blackboard*:)

A	B
1. He can _____.	1. He is very _____.
2. He is a good _____.	2. He is _____ than I am.

T: Under "A" I want you to take every word in list one and see if it fits in sentence 1. Then take every word in list two and see if it fits in sentence 2. Then take the words in list two that do fit in sentence 2, and list them under "A." Then you'll have a list A. Then we'll do the same with the sentences under "B," to make a list B. Let's try one example. Your first word in list one is what?

Ruth: "Work."

T: All right, let's try that in the first sentence under "A."

Ruth: "He can work."

T: Does it fit?

Ruth: Yes.

T: Okay. Now try the list-two word in the second sentence, Jane.

Jane: "He is a good worker."

T: Does that fit?

Jane: Yes.

T: So what would you put down here under your list "A"?

Children: "Worker."

T: Good. Now go ahead and do the rest. Then we'll see if we agree on the words when we get done.

(Children make lists.)

T: Are you all finished? . . . Now, Jane, would you read the words in your list "A," and the rest of you check and see if you agree with her?

Jane: "Worker," "runner," "helper," "singer," "fighter."

T: Do you agree, Joe?

Joe: Yes.

T: Does anybody disagree?

(No hands raised.)

T: My goodness. Ruth, would you read your words in list "B"?

Ruth: "Happier," "faster," "shorter," "sillier," and "fatter."

T: Do you agree with that list? Ira?

Ira: Uh huh.

T: Does anyone disagree?

(No hands.)

T: Why do you think we all agree on these lists "A" and "B," when we didn't agree on lists "X" and "Y"?

Ruth: Well, before we were talking about action words, and this time we were fitting words in sentences.

T: We may not be able to agree on what words show action, but we do agree on what words fit into these sentence patterns. That's very important to know. That's one reason why linguists don't talk about action words. They look at how words fit into sentences instead. Tomorrow we will see if we can figure out what kind of words we have in our second lists of "A" and "B." You might want to think about that in the meantime and see what ideas you can come up with.

EFFECTS OF INTERACTIVE DECISIONS

When confronted by children's use of the traditional grammarian's term "action words," this teacher decided to learn more about what children understood by this term, by having children list the "action words." The focus of the lesson then shifted to comparing two means of categorizing or grouping words, one being the use of a descriptive term, the other being the use of sentence patterns. The major objective of the lesson as it was conducted became the second objective: to show children a test they can use to determine whether a word ending in "er" is a noun or an adjective. The first, original objective—to have children see that the *er* ending is used to change verbs to nouns and also to form the comparative ending of adjectives—is postponed until the next day. An additional objective has been added, which is to have children realize that some tests or procedures for grouping words are more effective than others.

It is quite probable that the reader suggested another means of dealing with the problem of "action words." Many other alternatives are reasonable and effective within the framework of a discovery lesson.

The major problem that most teachers have in confronting an interactive decision during a discovery lesson is that their focus tends to shift to attainment of the "correct" or desired concept within the time period of the original lesson. In our model in Chapter 1 we have characterized the *secondary* objective of an inductive discovery lesson as the *eventual* attainment of the concept. Many attempts at discovery teaching fail because of the teacher's inability to make the split-second interactive decision, putting off attainment of the concept until a later time.

One way of evaluating your own simulated interactive decision in the foregoing lesson is to consider honestly the following questions:

1. Did you switch to a prescriptive or direct approach to correct children's misconceptions of "action words"?
2. Did you ignore the children's comments and move on with the original lesson plan regardless of their ideas about "action words"?

3. Did you try to get more information about what children meant by the term "action words"?
4. Did you give children more data to help them correct their own misconceptions about "action words"?

If you answered "yes" to questions 1 and 2 and "no" to questions 3 and 4, you are probably falling into the trap of making rapid attainment of the concept your primary objective. This will interfere with effective use of discovery strategies in interactive situations.

Regardless of your answers to the above questions, you may find it beneficial to get some additional practice in interactive decision making through classroom simulation. We suggest taping (audio or video) some of the discovery lessons you conduct in the classroom and having other teachers or education students with whom you work do the same. These lessons can then be played back to small study groups, stopped at "critical" points, and reacted to by different group members suggesting appropriate strategies or procedures for dealing with the immediate problem. This sharing of ideas can help to increase the "repertoire" of every group member.

chapter **17**

Classroom Management

Much has been written on classroom management and we have no strong urge to deal with it here except as discovery pedagogy affects management and as management affects discovery pedagogy. We should also like to make some suggestions to teachers who are big on individualized instruction, open classrooms, and contracts.

Management in a classroom is, in part, a function of whom one is teaching and what one is teaching. By whom one is teaching we do not mean Puerto Ricans, Mexicans, blacks, etc. To operate a successful classroom we must evaluate children in a number of areas. Factors other than cultural heritage are of importance in decisions about classroom management.

VARIABLES RELATED TO CLASSROOM MANAGEMENT

We may evaluate children in terms of their self-concepts as learners. Some feel and even verbalize that they are stupid. These children respond immediately to each new task with an "I can't do that" attitude. Other children feel they can attack and solve any task put before them.

Some children have rather good inquiry techniques and the ability to apply these techniques in novel situations. Other children have not as yet learned sound inquiry techniques. They rely heavily on guessing as a modus operandi.

Children vary in their ability to handle distractions. Some are easily distracted. Some persevere in the face of innumerable distractions.

Poor students are overwhelmed by tasks that appear too lengthy. They get anxious and are easily discouraged. Other children can conduct studies that extend over many days.

Some children view the indeterminate situation as a challenge to be resolved. The threatened or anxious child views indeterminacy as a situation to be avoided at all costs.

Children differ in the amount of knowledge and concepts they can bring to bear in a problematical situation. They also differ in their willingness to take risks and to try novel solutions.

Many children work well with other children in a cooperative fashion. Some work well with some children but not others. Some can only work when they are the leader, others only when they are followers.

Children also differ in their ability to work independently. Some children view the act of academic learning as being of value, others rarely view it as such.

Finally, children differ in that some must work almost constantly at the concrete manipulative level while others can work at the abstract level much of the time.

Each of these factors can be set up as a continuum, and a child could be evaluated in each area. The result would be a profile of characteristics such as Fig. 17–1. Children whose profiles are concentrated on the left present far fewer management problems than children whose profiles are concentrated on the right.

It is possible, of course, to develop a rating scale on each of the items in our list. We do not choose to work out the details of such a system at this point in time for several reasons. First, discerning teachers do not need a rating scale to measure whether or not a child is willing to attempt a new task or to determine if the child is easily distracted. Good teachers know what knowledge the child possesses, what mode of working is best for a child, and what techniques of inquiry he possesses. Second, a child who would be rated rather strongly in almost all characteristics in arithmetic may be rated on the other end of the scale in reading. Further, the same thing may hold within a particular subject area. A child who works with confidence, knowledge, independence, for lengthy periods of time, oblivious to all around him and taking great satisfaction in doing addition problems may well exhibit the opposite characteristics when working on fractions.

The characteristics a child exhibits are, then, a function of the situation. Behavior, as George Herbert Mead pointed out long ago, is situational. Given this, teachers would have to be constantly evaluating on rating scales and the time consumed would be enormous. Of course, if schools ever get around to hiring technicians to collect such data, we would have a situation in which teachers would constantly have up-to-date

	Self-Concept	
Positive		Negative
	Type of Rewards	
Internal		External
	Timing of Rewards	
Delayed		Immediate
	Interest	
High		Low
	Distractibility	
Low		High
	Tolerance of Indeterminacy	
High		Low
	Response to Long-term Studies	
Positive		Negative
	Willingness to Try the New	
High		Low
	Willingness to Work Independently	
High		Low
	Attitude Toward School Work	
Positive		Negative
	Control of Inquiry Techniques	
High		Low
	Knowledge	
High		Low
	Mode of Working	
Abstract		Concrete
	Ability to Work Cooperatively	
High		Low

Fig. 17–1 Profile of Management Variables

accurate data on each child. Data that would force more of us to face reality. But alas, we dream.

Several other observations relating to these characteristics should be noted. First, some of the characteristics are clustered variables while others are relatively independent variables. A child may have a very positive self-concept, sustain himself with internal rewards, be nondistractible, and feel very much at ease in an indeterminate situation as well as rate high on other characteristics, but completely lack the knowledge, mode of working, or inquiry skills necessary to proceed with a particular problem. These latter are independent variables.

High interest, on the other hand, will tend to reduce distractibility and the need for immediate and external rewards. Self-concept, type and timing of rewards, distractibility, interest, response to length of task, ability to handle indeterminacy and ambiguity, willingness to try something new, attitudes toward schoolwork, and the ability to work independently are clustered variables that interlock and overlap. Scores on these items will tend to be close together. Put another way, a child could score high on each of these but be rated very low on the independent variables. One shouldn't expect to find, however, a child scoring high on several of the clustered variables and very low on several of the other clustered variables.

INDIVIDUALIZING INSTRUCTION

Much of the literature on individualizing instruction focuses on the problem of differences in rate of learning. In the chapters on the structured inductive lesson (Chapters 9 and 10) and elsewhere in this book we have dealt with techniques for individualizing instruction within a group lesson, so that different children are provided with different amounts of data, or so that different children are dealing with different questions at the same time. The techniques we have suggested are strategies that help the teacher deal with children's differences in speed of arriving at a generalization.

What we are suggesting here is that there are many other types of individual differences that need to be considered in relation to the management of a classroom where discovery teaching occurs. The teacher must make decisions as to whether children will work alone or in groups, whether they will work independently or under supervision, whether they will have a small number or a large number of available alternatives. Attention to the characteristics noted on the Profile of Management Variables (Fig. 17–1) can help teachers make these kinds of decisions.

For example, it should be noted that children who are highly distractible will tend to have a low ability to work cooperatively. The group they are working in will provide a multitude of distractions simply because others are there. Other children may rate rather high on the clustered variables but not be able to work cooperatively because they have yet to learn the necessary skills. The child who lacks skills at working cooperatively but who scores high in the clustered variables should be allowed to work in a group with other children who rate high on the clustered variables but who also rate high in their ability to work cooperatively. In this setting the child will quickly learn the skills of working cooperatively by observing his peers.

Another child may rate rather low on all of the variables. A wide-open classroom with many options and one which requires a great deal of independence, skill, and self-assurance can be a desperate place for this child. This child needs a quiet place, somewhat isolated from others. He needs a highly structured lesson of the structured inductive type. He needs constant rewards from the teacher—often difficult to provide. One solution is to make sure that an adult passes near the child every minute or so to reward accomplishment. Another technique is to instruct the child to bring you his work as soon as he has completed x amount of work. The amount of work should be small. When the child presents the work to the teacher the teacher can indicate what is correct about the work and indicate any other things the child needs to do. The immediate reward and feedback tends to give this child a task he can handle, and the support he needs in order to work, while at the same time reducing his anxiety.

Children who rate in the middle of the scale and who are not easily distracted can take group instruction rather well. Teaching a large group is, of course, very efficient. The structured inductive discovery lesson or the semideductive discovery lesson work very well with these children. If they have skills in working cooperatively, group work is productive.

Children who rate high on the interlocking variables do well with the open inductive discovery lesson and can handle a great deal of freedom. For example, these children might be given the opportunity to rearrange part of the room along lines they feel will be most helpful to them in their work.

USE OF CONTRACTS

One method of individualizing instruction that has become fairly popular is the use of contracts. A *contract* is a written agreement between a teacher and a child that specifies a particular learning objective and a series of learning activities for the child to carry out independently. Frequently the contract also specifies the "reward" the child will receive upon completion of the contract. The reward usually takes the form of time during the school day for the child to engage in some particularly desirable activity.

Contracts may vary in length and complexity of activities involved. They may be completely planned and organized by the teacher, jointly planned by teacher and child, or completely planned by the child with approval by the teacher.

In classrooms where contracts are used the child who scores a low profile on the chart of management variables (Fig. 17–1) should not be given long-range contracts. Contracts for one or two hours' duration are long enough. Further, the teacher should present the child alternative contracts so that the child can accept either contract A or contract B. This gives the child some experience in decision making, but maintains some structure for him. The teacher should guard against letting this child talk him into grandiose plans which the child has no chance of completing, but for which he will fervently argue.

Children who score high on the dependent variables and high on inquiry techniques may be given the freedom to draw up their own contracts, and these contracts may be for one week's duration, or in some instances even longer. The longer and more complex the task, however, the more evidence the teacher must have that the child can organize his time and the higher rating on attitudes and internal rewards the child must have.

Many contracts presently in use in elementary school classrooms take the form of prescriptive lessons. Children are asked to read books on particular topics, to select pertinent facts, and to record them or report on them. The imaginative teacher can help children draw up contracts which involve more advanced inquiry techniques. A sample contract utilizing a discovery format appears below. This contract was planned cooperatively with both teacher and child contributing ideas.

Name	Susan G.
Date	January 27
Subject Area	Social Studies
Grade Level	Fourth

Specific Objective: To identify the most popular hobbies in the class.

Learning Outcome: A chart or graph showing how many children engage in each hobby. A minimum of five hobbies will be shown.

Learning Activities:

1. Interview each child in the class to find out what his or her favorite hobby is. Write down their answers. (Time—2 class periods)
2. Make a list of all the hobbies mentioned. Count the number of children who mentioned each hobby. (Time—1 class period)
3. Decide whether hobbies can be grouped to form types or categories of hobbies. (Time—1 class period)
4. Make a chart or graph to show the class. (Time—1 class period.) The chart will show:
   a. The types or categories of hobbies, if there are categories
   b. The number of children in the class who have each hobby

Learning Resources:

1. The children in the class
2. Paper and pencil
3. Oak tag or construction paper, ruler, paints or crayons

Expected Activity upon Completion of Contract: Susan will explain her hobby (knitting) to a group of interested classmates and show them things she has made.

RECORD KEEPING

Completed contracts and/or other work from the child who rates low on the clustered variables should be filed away. The teacher should note the amount of time the work took to complete, the child's resistance to doing it, and any other facts that may prove useful to convince a child that he is improving.

We often sit a child of this type down and have him compare the work he has done last week with the work he did ten or twenty weeks ago. The child will readily recall that he said it was too tough to do. He will deny that it took him ninety minutes to do "that easy work." One suspects that privately he is very pleased with his progress.

Moving from the low end to the high end of the scale is not a process of instant miracles. It is often a very slow, subtle process. Keeping a child's work in a folder gives the teacher and the child the data necessary to examine progress. Many children make the comment, "Did I do all of that?" and examine the work in mild disbelief, convinced they will find work in the folder that is not theirs. Then, impressed with what they have accomplished, they insist on completing all unfinished tasks. This they often do quite quickly, thereby furnishing further proof that they are growing as students. The reward in this activity is largely internal, as the child sees himself working with assurance, knowledge, and independence.

A child examining his folder (and one can have different folders for different subject areas or activities) is, of course, involved in an open discovery lesson in which he is learning about himself, his work, his attitudes toward work, and his teacher. These lessons are often very instructive and can lead to rather fruitful discussions between child and teacher. The following examples are excerpts from discussions in which we have participated.

SAMPLE DISCUSSIONS

Ten-year-old child: Boy, remember the trouble I had learning that?

Teacher: Yes. I also remember your saying you could never learn to do it.

Child: Yeah, I thought I was dumb.

T: I guess everyone thinks they are dumb sometimes.

Child: Nah—teachers never think they are dumb.

T: All the teachers I've known think they are dumb about some things.

Child: What do you do when you feel dumb about things?

T: Well, sometimes I fake it and act smart, and sometimes I try to avoid the problem by saying I don't really want to know about it. And sometimes I try to learn so I won't be dumb.

Child (after some silence): You know, children are a lot like teachers.

Nine-year-old boy: Boy, I had to work hard to get this good in minuses.

Teacher: Yes, you did.

Twelve-year-old boy: There is an awful lot of stuff here that isn't done.

Teacher: Yes, what do you think the problem is?

Boy: You.

T: Me? It's not my work.

Boy: Yes, but you're the teacher. You should make me work.

T: How can I make you work? Aren't you your own boss?

Boy: Yes, but you try to be too nice. You let me be too free. You have to keep me away from my friends. I need structure.

T: Structure? What's structure?

Boy: I'm not sure, but my mother says I need it.

Eight-year-old girl: Am I learning anything?

Teacher: Look at this addition paper in September and this one from yesterday. Do you think you're making progress?

Girl: Well, these problems seem harder.

T: They are.

Girl: But it seems that the work is always hard. It's never easy.

T: Why do you think that is so?

Girl: Because you give us hard work. You never give us easy work.

T: Learning to tell time was hard work. But you said you wanted to learn to tell time. I just helped. I didn't *make* you learn to tell time.

Girl: Well, I wanted to learn to tell time.

T: Why?

Girl: So I would know what time it was and people wouldn't laugh at me and call me dumb.

T: Okay, but why do you think it was hard to learn?

Girl: Because I'm dumb.

T: How can you say you were dumb? Dumb people don't learn. Only smart people learn. That's what it is to be smart. It's to learn. There must be another reason why you found it hard to learn. Maybe all learning is hard. Can you think of a reason why all learning is hard?

Girl: Because we don't know it already?

T: I think that might be right. Maybe that's why school work is hard. You're always trying to learn something new.

Child (heading outdoors to playground): My mother said she saw my folder and I was doing good work.

Teacher: Well, you looked at your folder. Do you think your mother is right?

Child: I guess so. (*Pause.*) Yes, I think so. (*Pause.*) Most of the time she's right. (*Pause.*) But I can do better than I'm doing. I've got to go now.

PARENT CONFERENCES

As the last discussion points up, another excellent use of these folders is in parent conferences. Having a parent look at dated records that show the child's work and progress from day to day accomplishes several things. First, it provides concrete data on which to base a discussion. Second, it develops parental trust in teachers because the teacher isn't hiding anything and because the parent can see the progress being made. Third, the child with a self-concept as a poor student has in all probability had that self-concept reinforced by his parents. If the parents look at the child's work, see progress, and then go home and tell the child that they see a great deal of improvement, this reinforcement pattern is broken and a more productive reinforcement pattern is introduced.

The parent-teacher conference can be a powerful tool in the hands of a competent teacher who recognizes that the child with a low profile needs all the help he can get. We once had a second-grade child who had previously been in a class for the mentally retarded (incorrect diagnosis) and who was on drugs (the 1960s' answer to most problems). During the course of the year he made considerable progress in math, some progress in reading, and some progress in behavior. In the March conference we suggested to the parents that perhaps we should take the child off drugs as he was often sleepy in class. The parents agreed. They further agreed to listen to the boy read each night for one half-hour. From that point on the boy blossomed as a student. He read with confidence and with a notable lack of distractibility and anxiety. He also began to win fist fights in the schoolyard that he had been losing. None of these events hurt his self-concept. The key in all of this rests, we think, with the conviction on the part of the parents that their child was not stupid. Consequently, they seemed willing to work with the child. This in turn helped convince the child he wasn't stupid and the child began to substitute "I can" for "I can't."

(We were not at all convinced a year later that we had done the right thing in suggesting that the parents take the child off the drugs. Having convinced them through the child's work that he was not stupid and was learning, we could have gotten the parents to listen to the boy read without playing doctor. With continued progress the parents themselves might have stopped the use of drugs. Perhaps they were already considering it. In any event, playing doctor is not our job. Neither is playing psychologist—but that is another tale.)

Besides the folder, the teacher has another device he may use at the parent-teacher conference. He can have the child perform some task recently learned. The effectiveness of this simple technique can easily be underestimated. Let us relate one story.

A mother who spoke no English came in with her non-English-reading but English-speaking third-grader during open house in early October. We suggested that her daughter read for us. The mother observed passively and without expression while her daughter read thirty words on chart 2 of "Words In Color."[1] Some of the words were read correctly immediately. Some the child stumbled over but then decoded successfully. The mother nodded her head and left. One day two weeks later the girl's reading group, under the direction of the student teacher, was making a great deal of noise. Just as the group was about to get out of hand our third-grade girl said to the group, "Be quiet. My mother says I should never fool around in reading. She says I'm going to learn to read this year and I am." It became a very hard working group from then on.

SELF-EVALUATION

The keeping of folders has another benefit. Individually and collectively the folders stand as testimony to the effectiveness or ineffectiveness of the teacher. A couple of days each summer spent with these folders can tell an intelligent teacher a great deal about what he is doing, how he is doing, and how effective he is with different children. Of course, they should be examined throughout the year as well.

1 For a description of this reading method see Harold Morine and Greta Morine, *A Primer for the Inner-City School* (New York: McGraw Hill Book Company, 1970), Chapter 8.

The keeping of individual folders, then, becomes a vehicle for collecting data on each child so that he and you can observe where he has been. It can be used so that you and he can jointly evaluate his progress and plan his work in the future. The evaluation should not only speak to the question of what knowledge has been learned and what skills have been mastered, but it should also address itself to the following questions:

Under what conditions do I work best?
Should I take on a little work at a time, or am I ready to take on big tasks?
Do I work best alone or in groups?
Can I handle distractions?
Where do my real interests lie?
What do I need to work on that doesn't interest me but that I need to know?

The teacher's self-evaluation can address itself to the following kinds of questions:

Have the children progressed as far as they might during this time period?
Are the instructional materials I have been giving them the best I can provide?
Am I helping them to become as independent as possible?
What problems do we still need to solve?

SELECTING WORK TO BE SAVED

Before leaving the problem of record keeping, let us briefly indicate some ideas for selecting work to be placed in the folders. The setting up of folders doesn't require a great deal of effort. Big manila envelopes with flaps that come down over the top are the best. One need not file all the work a child does. One strategy is to keep two folders. One is the permanent folder and one is the weekly folder. On Friday afternoon the child selects two pieces of work in each subject area from his weekly folder to place in his permanent folder. In selecting the two pieces of work the child selects his best and his worst. The teacher can, if he wishes, add one other piece of work to the child's folder. The work not selected for placement in the permanent folder may be taken home. Teachers may also place in the folder other information of a factual nature that seems significant. Some examples are:

It has been two days since Edward has been in a fight.
Mary had several excellent ideas in math today relating to multiplication.
A number of the children are copying Judy's style of painting.
Ramos worked for forty minutes today without interruption.
Today Peter got some insights on decoding.

One last word on folders. They should always be available for the child's perusal. They are a private record available to the teacher, the child, and the parent.

BE PREPARED

The most important part of managing a classroom to encourage discovery by children is to always be prepared. The kinds of preparations a teacher must make will vary at different times of the year.

Classrooms need constant restructuring. In September one may need many quiet, isolated carrels for children to work. In June few or none of these may be required. In the fall the physical structure of the classroom reflects the teacher's attempt to produce the most effective learning environment she can for the particular children she has. During the year it continually changes to reflect more and more the attempts of children to resolve problems they have perceived. More and more the room reveals the history of a group of children learning. A classroom should reflect the movement from a teacher-structured environment to a student-structured environment, from teacher-selected activities to student-selected activities.

To some extent this means that in the fall of the year the teacher must work much harder than in the spring. Planning in advance can be helpful. Children come into classrooms with widely differing knowledges in reading, math, art, language, etc. As we noted earlier, they differ also in self-concepts, interests, distractibility, etc. The teacher who is going to respond to these differences must be prepared with lessons of all the types we have described throughout this book, and many of these lessons must be developed prior to the start of the year. The alternative is to work four hours each night developing curriculum. Most commercial materials are useless to the sophisticated teacher. There is, of course, another alternative, and that is busy work. Sound discovery lessons take much thought and are difficult to plan under the pressure of time. The teacher who will spend an hour or two each day during the summer writing new lessons and rewriting lessons previously taught will be greatly rewarded during the following year.

Perhaps the most important part of being prepared is to understand the discovery process and to believe that it is valuable enough for you to exert the needed effort to make it work. If you have read this book carefully and carried out the suggested assignments, then you have taken a big step toward achieving that kind of preparedness.

We hope that you are now ready to accept the challenge of discovery, both for yourself and for the children with whom you work.

Self-Evaluation of Learning

The fourth part of this book has dealt with techniques for making discovery work on a long-term basis in the classroom. The only real evaluation of your learning here will result from your own analysis of your effectiveness in the classroom over an extended period of time. We hope you will make that evaluation, and that you will share what you learn with the teachers around you.

References

This is by no means an exhaustive list of references. It consists mainly of books we have found to be particularly useful in instructing students to use discovery methods and articles that report on relationships between classroom interaction patterns and children's learning.

DISCOVERY METHODS

COPELAND, RICHARD. 1970. *How Children Learn Mathematics.* New York: Macmillan.

JOYCE, BRUCE. 1971. *New Strategies for Social Education.* Chicago: Science Research Associates.

JOYCE, BRUCE AND MARSHA WEIL. 1972. *Models of Teaching.* Englewood Cliffs, N.J.: Prentice-Hall.

MORINE, HAROLD AND GRETA MORINE. 1970. *A Primer for the Inner-City School.* New York: McGraw-Hill.

SHULMAN, LEE AND EVAN KEISLAR. 1966. *Learning by Discovery: A Critical Appraisal.* Chicago: Rand McNally.

SMITH, E. BROOKS, KENNETH GOODMAN, AND ROBERT MEREDITH. 1970. *Language and Thinking in the Elementary School.* New York: Holt, Rinehart and Winston.

CLASSROOM INTERACTION

BELLACK, ARNO, ed. 1963. *Theory and Research in Teaching.* New York: Bureau of Publications, Teachers College, Columbia University.

COGAN, M. L. 1958. "The Behavior of Teachers and the Productive Behavior of Their Pupils: I.—'Perception' Analysis." *Journal of Experimental Education* 27:107–124.

CONNERS, C. K. AND L. EISENBERG. 1966. *The Effect of Teacher Behavior on Verbal Intelligence in Operation Headstart Children.* Baltimore: Johns Hopkins University School of Medicine (U.S. Office of Economic Opportunity Headstart Contract no. 510).

FLANDERS, NED. 1970. *Analyzing Teaching Behavior.* Reading, Mass.: Addison-Wesley.

FORTUNE, J. C. 1967. *A Study of the Generality of Presenting Behaviors in Teaching Pre-school Children.* Memphis: Memphis State University (U.S. Office of Education Project no. 6-8468).

HARRIS, A. J., C. MORRISON, B. L. SERWER, AND L. GOLD. 1968. *A Continuation of the Craft Project: Comparing Reading Approaches with Disadvantaged Urban Negro Children in Primary Grades.* New York: Division of Teacher Education of the City University of New York (U.S. Office of Education Project no. 5-0570-2-12-1).

HARRIS, A. J. AND B. SERWER. 1966. *Comparison of Reading Approaches in First Grade Teaching with Disadvantaged Children (the Craft Project).* New York: City University of New York (U.S. Office of Education Cooperative Research Project no. 2677).

MORINE, GRETA, ROBERT SPAULDING, AND SELMA GREENBERG. 1971. *Discovering New Dimensions in the Teaching Process.* Scranton: International Textbook Company.

MORRISON, B. M. 1966. "The Reactions of Internal and External Children to Patterns of Teaching Behavior." Ph.D. dissertation, University of Michigan.

PERKINS, H. V. 1951. "Climate Influences Group Learning." *Journal of Educational Research* 45:115–19.

SOAR, R. S. 1966. *An Integrative Approach to Classroom Learning.* Philadelphia: Temple University (Final Report, Public Health Service Grant no. 5-R11-MH 01096 and National Institute of Mental Health Grant no. 7-R11-MH 02045).

SPAULDING, R. L. 1963. *Achievement, Creativity, and Self-Concept Correlates of Teacher-Pupil Transactions in Elementary Schools.* Urbana, Illinois: University of Illinois (U.S. Office of Education Cooperative Research Project no. 1352).

WALLEN, N. E. 1966. *Relationships between Teacher Characteristics and Student Behavior—Part 3.* Salt Lake City: University of Utah (U.S. Office of Education Cooperative Research Project no. SAE OE5-10-181).

ANSWERS TO SELF-EVALUATION EXERCISES

<u>true</u> 1.   The student must use inductive thinking to arrive at the generalization or concept of what characterizes a Glig. He

<u>true</u> 2.   must use deductive thinking to apply the concept to the examples given at the end.

<u>false</u> 3.   This concept attainment exercise requires the student to use <u>convergent</u> thinking. (It is aimed at having all students arrive at the same concept.)

<u>false</u> 4.   In this exercise <u>inductive, convergent</u> thinking is followed by <u>deductive thinking</u>.

<u>true</u> 5.   Some students mark this false and argue that what is "sufficient" for one person may not be for another. This is a valid argument and should be counted correct.

<u>true</u> 6.

<u>false</u> 7.   The data are organized to promote attainment of <u>a single concept</u>. (All examples are together; all nonexamples are together.)

<u>true</u> 8.

<u>false</u> 9.   This concept attainment material is organized for an <u>indirect</u> teaching style. (The student must figure out the concept for himself; he is not told it. The examples do not *tell* him what the *characteristics* of a Glig are.)

<u>false</u> 10.   This concept attainment exercise is appropriate for <u>either individualized or group instruction</u>.

PART TWO

1. This lesson is an example of the semideductive discovery lesson. Children are using inductive thinking to arrive at a mathematical rule. The rule exists in a deductive system, and almost any data that can be selected will provide an example of the rule. (This was discussed in Chapter 6.)

2. Children must use the logical structure of combinativity in this lesson. They are combining two relationships ($A = B$ and $B = C$) in order to arrive at a new relationship ($A = C$). (This was discussed in Chapter 5.)

3. An important value that children might develop from use of this procedure is the attitude that immediate success is not an essential characteristic of problem-solving behavior. There are many alternative ways of stating this. (This was discussed in Chapter 5.)

PART THREE

Set   I. Open inductive lesson.

Set II. Structured inductive lesson.

Set III. Semideductive lesson.

Set IV. Transductive lesson.

Set V. Structured inductive lesson.

Index